KING ABDULLAH II

YASIR ARAFAT

BASHAR AL-ASSAD

MENACHEM BEGIN

SILVIO BERLUSCONI

TONY BLAIR

GEORGE W. BUSH

JIMMY CARTER

FIDEL CASTRO

RECEP TAYYIP ERDOĞAN

VICENTE FOX

SADDAM HUSSEIN

HAMID KARZAI

KIM IL SUNG and KIM JONG IL

HOSNI MUBARAK

PERVEZ MUSHARRAF

VLADIMIR PUTIN

MOHAMMED REZA PAHLAVI

ANWAR SADAT

THE SAUDI ROYAL FAMILY

GERHARD SCHROEDER

ARIEL SHARON

LUIZ INÁCIO LULA DA SILVA

MUAMMAR QADDAFI

MAJOR WORLD LEADERS

Luiz Inácio Lula da Silva

John Morrison

CHELSEA HOUSE
PUBLISHERS
A Haights Cross Communications Company

Philadelphia

Cover: The President of Brazil, Luiz Inácio Lula da Silva, waves at the crowd as he leaves the San Francisco church in Quito, during an official visit to Ecuador.

Frontispiece: Brazilian President Luiz Inácio Lula da Silva speaks after signing an agreement with his Chilean counterpart, Ricardo Lagos, at La Moneda presidential palace in Santiago, Chile.

CHELSEA HOUSE PUBLISHERS

V.P., NEW PRODUCT DEVELOPMENT Sally Cheney
DIRECTOR OF PRODUCTION Kim Shinners
CREATIVE MANAGER Takeshi Takahashi
MANUFACTURING MANAGER Diann Grasse

Staff for LUIZ INÁCIO LULA DA SILVA

EXECUTIVE EDITOR Lee Marcott
EDITORIAL ASSISTANT Carla Greenberg
PRODUCTION EDITOR Noelle Nardone
PICTURE RESEARCH Robin Bonner
INTERIOR DESIGN Takeshi Takahashi
COVER DESIGN Keith Trego
LAYOUT 21st Century Publishing and Communications, Inc.

A Haights Cross Communications ✦ Company

http://www.chelseahouse.com

First Printing

1 3 5 7 9 8 6 4 2

Library of Congress Cataloging-in-Publication Data

Morrison, John 1929–
    Luíz Inacio Lula da Silva / by John Morrison
       p. cm.—(Major world leaders)
Includes bibliographical references and index.
    ISBN 0-7910-8261-X (hardcover)
    1. Lula, 1945– —Juvenile literature. 2. Presidents—Brazil—Biography—Juvenile literature. 3. Brazil—Politics and government—1985—Juvenile literature. I. Title. II. Series.
F2538.5.L85M67 2004
981.06'5'092—dc22

                                                            2004017448

TABLE OF CONTENTS

On Leadership

Arthur M. Schlesinger, jr.

Leadership, it may be said, is really what makes the world go round. Love no doubt smoothes the passage; but love is a private transaction between consenting adults. Leadership is a public transaction with history. The idea of leadership affirms the capacity of individuals to move, inspire, and mobilize masses of people so that they act together in pursuit of an end. Sometimes leadership serves good purposes, sometimes bad; but whether the end is benign or evil, great leaders are those men and women who leave their personal stamp on history.

Now, the very concept of leadership implies the proposition that individuals can make a difference. This proposition has never been universally accepted. From classical times to the present day, eminent thinkers have regarded individuals as no more than the agents and pawns of larger forces, whether the gods and goddesses of the ancient world or, in the modern era, race, class, nation, the dialectic, the will of the people, the spirit of the times, history itself. Against such forces, the individual dwindles into insignificance.

So contends the thesis of historical determinism. Tolstoy's great novel *War and Peace* offers a famous statement of the case. Why, Tolstoy asked, did millions of men in the Napoleonic Wars, denying their human feelings and their common sense, move back and forth across Europe slaughtering their fellows? "The war," Tolstoy answered, "was bound to happen simply because it was bound to happen." All prior history determined it. As for leaders, they, Tolstoy said, "are but the labels that serve to give a name to an end and, like labels, they have the least possible connection with the event." The greater the leader, "the more conspicuous the inevitability and the predestination of every act he commits." The leader, said Tolstoy, is "the slave of history."

Determinism takes many forms. Marxism is the determinism of class. Nazism the determinism of race. But the idea of men and women as the slaves of history runs athwart the deepest human instincts. Rigid determinism abolishes the idea of human freedom—the assumption of free choice that underlies every move we make, every word we speak, every thought we think. It abolishes the idea of human responsibility, since it is manifestly unfair to reward or punish people for actions that are by definition beyond their control. No one can live consistently by any deterministic creed. The Marxist states prove this themselves by their extreme susceptibility to the cult of leadership.

More than that, history refutes the idea that individuals make no difference. In December 1931 a British politician crossing Fifth Avenue in New York City between 76th and 77th Streets around 10:30 P.M. looked in the wrong direction and was knocked down by an automobile—a moment, he later recalled, of a man aghast, a world aglare: "I do not understand why I was not broken like an eggshell or squashed like a gooseberry." Fourteen months later an American politician, sitting in an open car in Miami, Florida, was fired on by an assassin; the man beside him was hit. Those who believe that individuals make no difference to history might well ponder whether the next two decades would have been the same had Mario Constasino's car killed Winston Churchill in 1931 and Giuseppe Zangara's bullet killed Franklin Roosevelt in 1933. Suppose, in addition, that Lenin had died of typhus in Siberia in 1895 and that Hitler had been killed on the Western Front in 1916. What would the 20th century have looked like now?

For better or for worse, individuals do make a difference. "The notion that a people can run itself and its affairs anonymously," wrote the philosopher William James, "is now well known to be the silliest of absurdities. Mankind does nothing save through initiatives on the part of inventors, great or small, and imitation by the rest of us—these are the sole factors in human progress. Individuals of genius show the way, and set the patterns, which common people then adopt and follow."

Leadership, James suggests, means leadership in thought as well as in action. In the long run, leaders in thought may well make the greater difference to the world. "The ideas of economists and political philosophers, both when they are right and when they are wrong," wrote John Maynard Keynes, "are more powerful than is commonly understood. Indeed the world is ruled by little else. Practical men, who believe themselves to be quite exempt from any intellectual influences, are usually the slaves of some defunct economist. . . . The power of vested interests is vastly exaggerated compared with the gradual encroachment of ideas."

But, as Woodrow Wilson once said, "Those only are leaders of men, in the general eye, who lead in action. . . . It is at their hands that new thought gets its translation into the crude language of deeds." Leaders in thought often invent in solitude and obscurity, leaving to later generations the tasks of imitation. Leaders in action—the leaders portrayed in this series—have to be effective in their own time.

And they cannot be effective by themselves. They must act in response to the rhythms of their age. Their genius must be adapted, in a phrase from William James, "to the receptivities of the moment." Leaders are useless without followers. "There goes the mob," said the French politician, hearing a clamor in the streets. "I am their leader. I must follow them." Great leaders turn the inchoate emotions of the mob to purposes of their own. They seize on the opportunities of their time, the hopes, fears, frustrations, crises, potentialities. They succeed when events have prepared the way for them, when the community is awaiting to be aroused, when they can provide the clarifying and organizing ideas. Leadership completes the circuit between the individual and the mass and thereby alters history.

It may alter history for better or for worse. Leaders have been responsible for the most extravagant follies and most monstrous crimes that have beset suffering humanity. They have also been vital in such gains as humanity has made in individual freedom, religious and racial tolerance, social justice, and respect for human rights.

There is no sure way to tell in advance who is going to lead for good and who for evil. But a glance at the gallery of men and women in MAJOR WORLD LEADERS suggests some useful tests.

One test is this: Do leaders lead by force or by persuasion? By command or by consent? Through most of history leadership was exercised by the divine right of authority. The duty of followers was to defer and to obey. "Theirs not to reason why/Theirs but to do and die." On occasion, as with the so-called enlightened despots of the 18th century in Europe, absolutist leadership was animated by humane purposes. More often, absolutism nourished the passion for domination, land, gold, and conquest and resulted in tyranny.

The great revolution of modern times has been the revolution of equality. "Perhaps no form of government," wrote the British historian James Bryce in his study of the United States, *The American Commonwealth*, "needs great leaders so much as democracy." The idea that all people should be equal in their legal condition has undermined the old structure of authority, hierarchy, and deference. The revolution of equality has had two contrary effects on the nature of leadership. For equality, as Alexis de Tocqueville pointed out in his great study *Democracy in America*, might mean equality in servitude as well as equality in freedom.

"I know of only two methods of establishing equality in the political world," Tocqueville wrote. "Rights must be given to every citizen, or none at all to anyone . . . save one, who is the master of all." There was no middle ground "between the sovereignty of all and the absolute power of one man." In his astonishing prediction of 20th-century totalitarian dictatorship, Tocqueville explained how the revolution of equality could lead to the *Führerprinzip* and more terrible absolutism than the world had ever known.

But when rights are given to every citizen and the sovereignty of all is established, the problem of leadership takes a new form, becomes more exacting than ever before. It is easy to issue commands and enforce them by the rope and the stake, the concentration camp and the *gulag*. It is much harder to use argument and achievement to overcome opposition and win consent. The Founding Fathers of the United States understood the difficulty. They believed that history had given them the opportunity to decide, as Alexander Hamilton wrote in the first Federalist Paper, whether men are indeed capable of basing government on "reflection and choice, or whether they are forever destined to depend . . . on accident and force."

Government by reflection and choice called for a new style of leadership and a new quality of followership. It required leaders to be responsive to popular concerns, and it required followers to be active and informed participants in the process. Democracy does not eliminate emotion from politics; sometimes it fosters demagoguery; but it is confident that, as the greatest of democratic leaders put it, you cannot fool all of the people all of the time. It measures leadership by results and retires those who overreach or falter or fail.

It is true that in the long run despots are measured by results too. But they can postpone the day of judgment, sometimes indefinitely, and in the meantime they can do infinite harm. It is also true that democracy is no guarantee of virtue and intelligence in government, for the voice of the people is not necessarily the voice of God. But democracy, by assuring the right of opposition, offers built-in resistance to the evils inherent in absolutism. As the theologian Reinhold Niebuhr summed it up, "Man's capacity for justice makes democracy possible, but man's inclination to justice makes democracy necessary."

A second test for leadership is the end for which power is sought. When leaders have as their goal the supremacy of a master race or the promotion of totalitarian revolution or the acquisition and exploitation of colonies or the protection of greed and privilege or the preservation of personal power, it is likely that their leadership will do little to advance the cause of humanity. When their goal is the abolition of slavery, the liberation of women, the enlargement of opportunity for the poor and powerless, the extension of equal rights to racial minorities, the defense of the freedoms of expression and opposition, it is likely that their leadership will increase the sum of human liberty and welfare.

Leaders have done great harm to the world. They have also conferred great benefits. You will find both sorts in this series. Even "good" leaders must be regarded with a certain wariness. Leaders are not demigods; they put on their trousers one leg after another just like ordinary mortals. No leader is infallible, and every leader needs to be reminded of this at regular intervals. Irreverence irritates leaders but is their salvation. Unquestioning submission corrupts leaders and demeans followers. Making a cult of a leader is always a mistake. Fortunately hero worship generates its own antidote. "Every hero," said Emerson, "becomes a bore at last."

The signal benefit the great leaders confer is to embolden the rest of us to live according to our own best selves, to be active, insistent, and resolute in affirming our own sense of things. For great leaders attest to the reality of human freedom against the supposed inevitabilities of history. And they attest to the wisdom and power that may lie within the most unlikely of us, which is why Abraham Lincoln remains the supreme example of great leadership. A great leader, said Emerson, exhibits new possibilities to all humanity. "We feed on genius. . . . Great men exist that there may be greater men."

Great leaders, in short, justify themselves by emancipating and empowering their followers. So humanity struggles to master its destiny, remembering with Alexis de Tocqueville: "It is true that around every man a fatal circle is traced beyond which he cannot pass; but within the wide verge of that circle he is powerful and free; as it is with man, so with communities." ▪

1

The Workers' President

H e was the people's man, and this was their day. New Year's Day 2003 brought more than 200,000 people to Brasília, the shining modern capital of Brazil, for the inauguration of Luiz Inácio Lula da Silva. Known to everyone as "Lula," he was the first member of the working class to become president of this vast nation of 175 million people. And the working people turned out to cheer him, in a nearly hysterical display of rejoicing that at last someone who knew their pain, because he had felt it himself, was their leader. Crowds danced the samba and waved flags and banners in a show of joy usually reserved for the country's frequent victories in World Cup soccer.

Lula, the onetime shoeshine boy and fiery labor leader, who once resembled a chubby Lenin haranguing the crowds in a T-shirt and jeans, had cleaned up his image and moderated the left-wing

President Lula da Silva and his wife Marisa wave as they ride in an open car in Brasília after Lula's swearing-in ceremony as president of Brazil, January 1, 2003. Da Silva, who dropped out of school as a boy to shine shoes and went on to become the leader of Brazil's leftist Workers' Party, was inaugurated as the thirty-sixth president of Latin America's biggest nation.

views that had frightened Brazil's elite as well as international bankers. The boy who was born into poverty, who didn't learn to read until he was 10 and never attended high school, now rode in an open Rolls-Royce through leaping and waving throngs shouting his name.

Many revelers were wrapped in the green and yellow Brazilian flag, as well as the deep red of Lula's Workers' Party banner. They splashed through the pools that surround the capital buildings, heedless of getting soaked. One man almost pulled

Lula out of his car as he tried to embrace him. The hooves of the horses of the white-uniformed Dragoons of Independence, a mounted military guard established in 1808 by King João VI, clattered on the pavement beside the convertible. The Rolls-Royce was a gift from the Queen of England in the 1950s to Getúlio Vargas, then Brazil's president.

Lula, who was 57, looked like a distinguished, well-fed banker in his dark suit and tie, his salt-and-pepper beard neatly trimmed. His attractive second wife, Marisa Letícia, was at his side. His appearance alone might have been enough to reassure the wary that Lula was no longer a wild-eyed radical and that they had nothing to fear.

CASTRO ARRIVES

Leaders of 119 countries attended the inauguration. Among the guests were fellow leftists, Fidel Castro, the president of Cuba, and Hugo Chávez, the president of Venezuela. (People on the political "left" tend to favor radical or liberal causes, whereas those on the "right" favor more conservative or traditional policies.) President George W. Bush was one of the first to congratulate Lula on his election victory. Trade Representative Robert B. Zoellick was sent to represent the United States at the ceremony.

After Lula and his vice president, José Alencar, took the oath of office in the National Congress building, the legislators shouted, "Olé, olé, olé, ola Lula," and sang the national anthem. Eager crowds pushed through the police barricades and ran across the grassy bank outside the building. Many watched the inauguration ceremony on large TV screens that had been put up around the city.

A group of nuns squeezed through the crowds to get a look at the new leader. "For us this is a historic moment for our country," Sister Maria da Conceicao was quoted as saying by Agence France-Presse. "We are a rich nation debased by corruption, and we hope the new government will bring a new outlook for the Brazilian people, a wonderful people who have suffered heavily under unjust policies."

The British Broadcasting Corporation (BBC) reported the reaction of Jason Ferreira, who was part of the cheering crowd. "Since 1500 an exploiting elite has governed Brazil," he said. "The people have dreamed of this."

In his inaugural speech, Lula proclaimed, "I am not the result of one election, I am the result of a history. I am realizing the dreams of generations and generations before me who tried and failed."

AN END TO HUNGER

Lula was elected with a convincing 61 percent of the vote on his fourth try for the presidency. He rode to victory with a promise to "transform Brazil." He vowed to end hunger, poverty, and corruption. "If at the end of my mandate, all Brazilians have the chance to eat breakfast, lunch, and dinner, I will have fulfilled the mission of my life," he said in his inaugural address.

If he was going to transform Brazil, he had his work cut out for him. Brazil was $260 billion in debt to foreign nations when he took office, and the international banking community had feared a default (failure to pay debts) similar to one that crippled neighboring Argentina a short time before. Unemployment was high, inflation was hurting families because wages were low, crime was rampant, mostly because of the growing drug trade, education was inadequate, and government corruption was an embarrassment.

But the worst problem–one that had confounded Brazil's leaders for generations–was the great discrepancy between the haves and the have-nots. Some 58 million people lived in poverty–on less than $1 a day. People who had jobs were not doing much better. One-third of Brazil's population was living below the poverty line–making about 79 *reals* ($27) a month. (The *real* is Brazil's basic currency). Which means simply that most Brazilians are poor.

As Lula prepared to take office, the question in the minds of many observers was, as it always has been, was Brazil governable at all?

It is a huge nation, nearly as large as the United States. If you wanted to travel from the northern border where the Amazon Basin is to the farthest southern point at the border with Uruguay, you would have to cover 2,684 miles (4,319 km). Going east to west, from the Atlantic Ocean to the border with Peru, you would cover 2,689 miles (4,328 km).

And in this huge land you would encounter a great diversity of people, from the farmers and ranchers of the "backlands" to the dwellers of the big cities on the coast, where the great bulk of the population lives. You can easily imagine that the "beautiful people" on the famous beaches of Copacabana and Ipanema have little or nothing in common with the farmers, the cattle-herding gauchos, and the rubber-tappers and coffee growers of the interior. And certainly the people of the *favelas*, the slums, which look down on the wonders of Rio de Janeiro and the other magnificent cities, have nothing in common with their fellow citizens below.

THE DIVERSE NATION

And what is a Brazilian anyway? Slightly more than half of the people are of European descent—Germans, Italians, Poles, Portuguese, Spaniards. About 6 percent are of African descent, and 38 percent are of mixed African and European heritage. One percent are Indians, who live mostly in the Amazon regions.

Brazil is more than coffee, which once accounted for more than 50 percent of its agricultural exports. That figure is down to about 5 percent today. The lyrics of a song stick in old-timers' minds—"There's an awful lot of coffee in Brazil."

It is more than Carmen Miranda, who personified Brazil to Americans as the star of popular musicals in the '40s. (Many Brazilians resented Miranda's depiction of a Brazilian as she

A rural worker collects coffee beans at a farm near Varginha, in the state of Minas Gerais. The 2003 harvest, shown here, produced a record amount of exportable coffee because of lack of a frost that year, which usually destroys much of the crop. Coffee is one of Brazil's chief exports.

wore silly headdresses made of fruit while she danced and sang in a thick accent that was supposed to be funny.)

Brazil is more than soccer and Pelé. More than Carnival, and string bikinis on Copacabana Beach, and the "girl from Ipanema." It is more than the Brazilian millionaire who fell in love with Audrey Hepburn in "Breakfast at Tiffany's." And it is more than the Amazon and the rain forest.

Much has been written about the Brazilian character. Driving through the streets of Rio or São Paulo or any other big city, you take your life in your hands. Brazilians have a serious disregard for traffic lights and stop signs—and speed limits. Traffic fatalities are among the highest in the world.

Brazilians can obsess over soccer, which they call football. More than 200,000 fans jam Maracana Stadium in Rio, one of the world's largest, to watch matches. For decades, Brazilians pondered, analyzed, and brooded over the loss of a World Cup game to Uruguay in 1950, a game that Brazil was supposed to win easily. Soccer victories, especially in the World Cup, cause nationwide euphoria, and losses can plunge the entire country into the worst of depressions. There have been suicides of fans who could not bear to continue living knowing their team had lost an important match.

It has been said that every Brazilian child goes to sleep with a soccer ball under his bed, even though the National Basketball Association has made recent inroads into the Brazilian passion for soccer. Several Brazilians play on NBA teams in the United States, and their countrymen follow their exploits on television. Lula was a devoted soccer player himself, and continued to have matches among staff members on the capital lawn after he became president.

The antics of the annual Carnival in the big cities are world famous. Half-naked (and some completely naked) men and women lose total control of themselves in the revelry leading up to the start of Lent. Accompanied by a thundering samba beat, the frenzy of Carnival marchers can take on an orgiastic cast. People spend an entire year preparing for their participation in the parades.

GOD'S LITTLE JOKE

A man who helped organize Carnival celebrations once commented, "If you consider the planet as a living entity, Brazil is its heart, thus Brazil's function is to bring happiness to this earth."

Brazil is a beautiful, lush country with a delightfully warm climate.

There is a joke that Brazilians tell on themselves: An angel complained to God that He wasn't being fair in putting so much natural beauty in one country and keeping it free of natural disasters like hurricanes and floods. God replied, "Ah, but wait till you see the people I'm going to put there."

It has been said that Brazil is not a serious country. If you want to try to figure out what makes a Brazilian tick, think of a child of about 5, with all the excesses and temperament and fantasies and annoyances of childhood, but with so many endearing qualities that you cannot help loving him.

The dark side of the Brazilian character has emerged, too, in a number of well-publicized brutal actions, like the murder of eight street children, shot to death as they slept, probably by policemen, in 1993. Brazil has one of the world's highest murder rates, and it has been written that Brazilians do not respect human life as people in other countries do.

There is a great worship of youth and beauty. In recent years, plastic surgeons have been elevated to the level of heroes, even gods, by middle-aged people trying to recapture their youth. The beautiful people who wear their famous skimpy bathing suits on the beaches must look terrific—as long as nature and the surgeon's scalpel will allow.

WHAT WENT WRONG?

For centuries, Brazilians have been baffled over why their

country is not great. In some ways, its history paralleled that of the United States, beginning as a colony of a foreign country.

Brazil has the size, the natural resources, the willing workers. But, while the United States developed into the world's greatest superpower, Brazil is still struggling to identify itself, and to cope with problems it has failed to solve since it gained independence from Portugal in 1822.

Every president from Marshal Deodoro da Fonseca, who established the republic and put forth the first Constitution in 1891, to Luiz Inácio Lula da Silva have declared their intention to make Brazil a great country, to wrest it kicking and screaming into the future. It has had eight constitutions (the basic law of the land that establishes the government), while the United States has gotten along on one, however many times it has been amended.

But hope rises with every new change of government. Maybe this time . . . , the people say. But every regime has ended in disappointment.

Now, it is Lula's turn. Not long after his inauguration, he cautioned the people not to expect miracles. (This to a people who believe in miracles!) He warned that his program of reform would probably take more time than his first four-year term. He is already thinking about reelection in 2006.

But on that New Year's Day in 2003, the people's enthusiasm was understandable. For the first time in Brazilian history, a man from the working class, who had known the desperation of poverty, who knew what it was like to struggle for a living, who even knew—in 1980—what it was like to be arrested and slapped into jail, was going to lead the country.

As always, Brazilians celebrated with music.

A huge open-air concert featuring some of the country's leading pop musicians was held before the inauguration. Gilberto Gil, one of Brazil's most popular singers and song-writers, started the program with chants of "Viva Lula!"

The Reuters news agency quoted Ana Lucia Marques da Silva (no relation), 45, from Lula's home state of Pernambuco, as saying, "There has never been a popular outpouring like this for a president, and that is because he is a worker."

Lula's friendship with Fidel Castro, Cuba's Communist leader, could not have sat well with the American government, which has been trying to oust Castro since shortly after he took over. But Castro was an honored guest at the inauguration. "It is a very happy day for me, because January 1 has always been an important day for the Cuban people," said Castro, who overthrew the government on New Year's Day 1959. "And now, January 1 will be an important day for the people of Brazil."

THE GREAT FUTURE

In his inauguration speech, Lula called Brazil "a country that never ceases to be young and new."

"These people know the meaning of suffering," he went on, "but at the same time know the meaning of happiness. These people believe in themselves and in their own strength.

"I believe that a great future awaits Brazil because our happiness is bigger than our pain, our strength is bigger than our misery, and our hope is bigger than our fears."

He insisted that he meant it when he used the word "change." "That is the key word," he said. "That was the message that Brazilian society delivered during the October election. Hope finally defeated fear, and society decided that this was the time to walk new roads."

The idea of change, though, did not please many members of the elite, who had long ruled Brazil from behind the scenes, or the business and banking leaders, the stock brokers, and many conservative political leaders. When it looked like Lula was going to win the election, the stock market dropped and some bankers even said they planned to leave the country. They were soothed by Lula's change of tone.

"We are going to change, yes," he told his audience. "We are going to change with courage, but carefully. We will be humble

President Luiz Inácio Lula da Silva poses with governors of all states of the country before meeting in Brasília, February 21, 2003, shortly after da Silva's inauguration. President da Silva called the governors together to discuss tax and social security reforms.

and daring. We will change, but at the same time we know that it is a gradual and continuous process and not just a simple expression of will."

Those were words the conservatives were happy to hear.

Lula also promised to fight corruption in government, tax evasion by the rich, government waste, inflation, unemployment, and low wages. But his main thrust, expressed in his inauguration speech and during his campaign, was the elimination of hunger.

"This is a country that has so much fertile land and so many people who want to work that there is no reason to talk about hunger," he said. "Millions of Brazilians inside and outside the cities, however, lack food today. They survive, miraculously, under the poverty line, if they do not die while begging for a piece of bread.

"This is an old story. . . . This situation cannot continue. As long as one of our Brazilian brethren is hungry, we have enough reason to be embarrassed."

The man who once sold oranges in the street and worked as a shoeshine boy to help his family knew what he was talking about.

2

The Rise
of Lula

Talk about a man who wouldn't give up. Luiz Inácio Lula da Silva was that man. He lost three elections for president, and one for the governorship of a state. But he was undaunted. He kept coming back and finally captured the presidency in 2002.

Lula began the union activities that would ultimately lead him into politics in the early 1970s. Brazil was then in the midst of the brutal 21-year military dictatorship that began in 1964. Union activities were severely restricted; strikes were illegal; and the government could intervene whenever it didn't like what a union was doing. The more militant leaders, including eventually Lula himself, were arrested.

It took the young Lula some time to become involved in any activities outside of his own life. He was never much interested in politics in his youth. In 1969, he married a woman who worked in a

Luis Inácio Lula da Silva, founder of the Workers' Party, speaks to the crowd during his bid for governor of São Paulo, in 1984. As a union organizer in a country where strikes are illegal, he is often compared to Poland's Lech Walesa.

textile factory. She died two years later during childbirth. The son she was delivering did not survive either. There were other romances as well, and, besides, Lula was too busy playing soccer.

It took Lula's brother, José, a committed member of the Communist Party, to get him interested in the problems of the workers. By then, Lula was a metalworker in a large factory in São Bernardo do Campo, just outside São Paulo.

The Communist Party was illegal at the time and was operating secretly. José, who was known as Frei (Friar) Chico because his haircut made him look like a monk, was finally able to lure his brother off the soccer field long enough to join the local metalworkers' union. (Communism, which has never existed in its pure form in the world, holds that nations should be run by the *proletariat*—the workers—and that, eventually, the government will wither away. Communist countries, however, have never been much more than dictatorships.)

HE'S ONE OF THEM

Through much of Brazil's modern history, union leaders tended to be more like bureaucrats than workers. They had little in common with the rank-and-file members and, therefore, were not always willing to fight for their rights. Lula had no such problem. He was one of the workers. He spoke their language and understood their concerns.

He soon found he enjoyed union work and decided to run for office. In 1975, he won the presidency of the Metalworkers' Union of São Bernardo do Campo and Diadema. The union had a membership of about 100,000. He was reelected three years later.

Lula also found that he had a flair for public speaking, though he had a slight lisp. During this period, he became one of the leading spokesmen for the Brazilian labor movement. Newspapers and television stations covered his speeches extensively. Here was a labor leader who was also a worker. Most unusual for Brazil.

The so-called Brazilian miracle under the military dicta-torship was a period of spectacular growth in the early 1970s. Industrial development boomed. Factories around São Paulo were turning out automobiles and automotive parts. The workforce expanded, and skilled workers saw their wages grow so they could actually buy some of those cars.

One reason for the boom was that employers could run their businesses how they wanted without worrying about union problems. For instance, some of them forced their workers to increase productivity to the extent that industrial accidents rose. Pollution was out of control. And the unions were helpless to do anything.

Unfortunately, the "miracle" didn't last. The oil crisis of 1973, when the Organization of Petroleum Exporting Countries (OPEC) raised prices because of Middle East conflicts, brought it to a halt. Brazil needed foreign oil to keep its factories going.

Prices shot up, but wages didn't keep pace. One of Lula's early battles came as the result of a government swindle. To try to show that inflation was not as bad as it was, the govern-ment issued phony inflation figures. Since wage increases (the government set a minimum wage) were supposed to keep up with inflation, the workers were, therefore, being cheated out of the salary increases they deserved.

The unions, led by the Metalworkers, embarked on a "wage restoration" campaign, to try to force the government to boost salaries. Although strikes were illegal, the workers engaged in slowdowns and sit-down strikes. In such activities, employees show up for work, but either slow their production, or sit on the floor or on machinery, preventing any work from being done. It was estimated that in 1979, as many as three million workers in Brazil engaged in some kind of strike activity.

A DIFFERENT IDEA

The military leaders were by now anxious to restore democracy to Brazil, but the generals realized that change would have to be introduced slowly. One of their first steps was to do away with the artificial two-party system they had introduced to make it look as if democratic principles were being followed. They agreed to allow multiple parties, but this move was not expected to have much impact. Brazilian tradition held that the name of the party you belonged to didn't mean much. The parties were generally all out for themselves, without much concern for ideology or principle.

However, Lula and other young labor leaders had different ideas. They wanted to form a political party that would actually stand for something, a party that would truly represent the people it was supposed to. And so the Workers' Party was born. In Portuguese, the name is Partido dos Trabalhadores, thus giving the party its customary designation as "PT."

The PT was unique in Brazilian history because it was formed by workers to represent workers, rather than being formed by politicians who merely pretended to speak for the workers. The party was originally based in the industrialized regions in and around São Paulo, but gradually spread to other parts of the country.

Its principles were basically socialist. Although many kinds of socialism are at work in the world, socialists generally believe that the means of production, as well as land, transportation, and other sectors, should be owned by the government. The PT did not care for foreign models of socialism. It also rejected any alliance with the Brazilian Communist Party, which was asserting itself under the new freedoms permitted by the military.

The generals didn't like either group. "Troublemakers" were removed from party leadership. Lula and other union leaders were arrested in 1980 for instigating a strike in the auto industry. A military court sentenced him to three and a half years in prison. There was immediate outrage among the people. Protesters marched in the streets. The military backed down, and a higher court threw out the sentence. Lula

Honorary chairperson of the Workers' Party (PT) and main opposition leader, Lula da Silva, sits with a red rose handed out in Congress in Brasília in this May 9, 2001 photo. At the time, da Silva was leading the polls for the October 2001 presidential election, with 30 percent of the vote. It was his fourth presidential bid.

emerged from prison to a hero's welcome. His popularity was growing everywhere. His arrest only added to his fame.

In 1982, he ran as the PT candidate for governor of the state of São Paulo. Victory seemed to be in the bag. Party rallies attracted large crowds, with the main message being, "Worker, vote for a worker."

But the Workers' Party was in for a shock. Lula received only 10 percent of the vote and came in fourth. What happened?

Analysts believe that Lula was just too much of a worker for the workers. They knew *they* couldn't run a government, so how could Lula, if he was one of them? People who run governments have to have college educations, and are probably wealthy. They go around in suits and ties, not T-shirts and jeans.

The PT learned valuable lessons from the debacle. The party realized that it needed to broaden its base to include more than just factory workers. It got rid of its "Worker, vote for a worker" slogan. People who were not urban workers were nominated as candidates for local elections. The party also softened its angry rhetoric, and started to make more use of television.

THE PT MAKES PROGRESS

The 1982 election results were not all bad. The PT gained stature among the voters by electing six candidates to the national Chamber of Deputies, and nine to the legislature of São Paulo state. (Brazil's Congress consists of an 81-member Senate and a 513-member Chamber of Deputies. It is similar to the United States Congress, which consists of a Senate and a House of Representatives.)

The PT was rolling along. In 1986, Lula won 650,000 votes and became a member of the Chamber of Deputies. He got more votes than any other candidate in the country. That year, the party put up candidates for mayor in all but one state capital and did well. A PT member became mayor of Fortaleza, in the state of Ceara in the northeastern part of the country.

An example of how broad-based the party had become was the election of Benedita da Silva, a black community activist from the notorious *favela* in Rio de Janeiro, to the Chamber of Deputies. (Silva is a common name in Brazil, similar to Smith and Jones in the United States.)

Benedita had an interesting history. She was one of 13 children born to a poverty-stricken family. She often had to pick through rubbish bins to find food. She later became an activist against racism and poverty, and led community development meetings and women's rights protests. In her spare time, she took university courses.

In 1994, she became the first black woman elected to the Senate. After he became president, Lula named her to his cabinet as minister of social development.

The Workers' Party was rapidly gaining the reputation of being the only political party in Brazil that actually believed in something. In 1988, the party did even better in the mayoral races, capturing the city halls of Porto Alegre; Vitoria, the capital of the state of Espirito Santo; and the cities of Campinas and Santos in São Paulo state. PT candidate Luiza Erundina, a social worker, won a surprising victory over Paulo Maluf for the important post of mayor of São Paulo, one of the world's largest cities.

But one problem the PT faced was that it started out as a party in opposition. It fought against military rule; it fought against capitalism; it fought against what it saw as international interference in Brazil's affairs; and it fought against everything else it thought kept workers down.

THE PARTY CHANGES

Once the military dictatorship ended in 1985, the PT found it had to supplement its negative stances with some positive positions. It also came to realize that even though other political parties were not so ideologically pure, the PT had to form alliances with them to increase its influence. The party could no longer be as standoffish as it was in 1985, when it refused to support the popular presidential candidacy of Tancredo Neves. Neves was elected, but died at age 75 before he could assume office.

In 1989, the party nominated Lula as its presidential candidate. His chances seemed good since his opponents were rather lackluster. One candidate whom Lula despised was Leonel Brizola, brother-in-law of João Goulart, the former president who was forced into exile when the military took over in 1964. Lula said Brizola "would step on his own mother's neck to get elected."

A stronger candidate was Fernando Collor de Mello, a young, charismatic former governor of the state of Alagoas. He came from a wealthy family, and supporters hailed him as another John F. Kennedy.

In the first round of voting, Collor won easily with 28 percent of the vote. Lula, who received 16 percent of the vote, narrowly edged the hated Brizola for the runner-up position by some 450,000 votes out of 72 million cast. Since Collor did not win an absolute majority, as required by the Constitution, he had to face a runoff with the second-place finisher, Lula.

The second campaign was marked by smear tactics by Collor's supporters. They brought out Lula's former lover who claimed on national television that he had urged her to abort their daughter. Actually, Collor himself had fathered an illegitimate child, but that was not revealed until after the election. Using his family money to bolster his campaign funds, Collor saturated the country with TV and newspaper ads, and was able to pay hundreds of campaign workers to get out the vote for him.

Despite the PT's socialist agenda, Lula had promised that he would use no foreign models in his government. It was a time when the Soviet Union was collapsing and Communist regimes in Eastern Europe were coming apart. Some accusations were made that the PT was going against the tide of world history.

NOT ENOUGH TO WIN

But Lula insisted he favored privatization of certain state-held entities, though the government should continue to own the power and oil industries. He said the government should have a strong hand in forming industrial development policies. No one seemed particularly frightened by the extreme left-wing members of the Workers' Party, who advocated more radical policies.

Lula had the satisfaction of getting 31 million of his country-men to vote for him, but it was not enough to win. Collor became president in March 1990.

Brazilians had been shaken by the death of the popular Tancredo Neves on the eve of his inauguration in 1985, and the elevation of the lackluster José Sarney, the vice president. Sarney, the first civilian president after the military dictatorship ended, was not a complete failure. His economic policies worked for a while, but when he made some missteps, inflation soared out of control. The people were ready for a "John F. Kennedy" to lead them to prosperity. But it didn't happen.

When Collor took over, he inherited a $90 billion debt that was a legacy of the military government's reckless spend-ing. He declared a national emergency and issued a number of controversial decrees to correct the problem. He froze savings accounts and prices. Businesses had their operating capital frozen. People who had made purchases, like houses and autos, found they could not access their bank accounts.

Collor had promised to shrink government, and laid off thousands of federal workers, contributing to the unemployment problem. He reduced tariffs (the fees paid by foreign companies to bring their products into the country) on many goods, but manufacturers were not given any time to meet the ensuing foreign competition.

He had also promised to attack government corruption, but a bribery scandal soon racked his administration. A congres-sional investigation began, and an impeachment vote passed.

Totally discouraged by his failures, Collor decided to resign rather than be kicked out. Nevertheless, the Senate voted 76 to 5 to remove him from office and strip him of political rights for eight years. The senators were very angry. (As in the United States, the lower house of Congress—in Brazil, the Chamber of Deputies—can impeach a president, or any other public official, who is then tried in the Senate.)

NUCLEAR PACT

One accomplishment of the Collor administration was to bring an end to nuclear competition with Argentina. The two countries agreed on a non-nuclear proliferation pact and began to cooperate on conventional weapons development. It was not known how far either country had gotten toward developing nuclear weapons, but both nations were working on them.

Another accomplishment was the signing of an agreement to form a regional trading group with Argentina, Uruguay, and Paraguay called Mercosul. (One dream of South American leaders, including Lula, has been the eventual creation of a South American common market, in which member countries would pool their resources and talents to establish a powerful trading group. The model is the European Common Market. So far, the dream has been elusive in Latin America.)

After Collor quit in December 1992, Vice President Itamar Franco took over. The best thing Franco did was to appoint Fernando Henrique Cardoso, a prominent academic and a senator from São Paulo, to lead the Finance Ministry in 1993. Cardoso, who would go on to serve eight years as president, brought in a team of experts to help revive the Brazilian economy.

They had a mess on their hands. Inflation had reached 2,103.7 percent. It would reach 2,406.8 percent the next year. People were suffering. The Cardoso team introduced the Real Plan, establishing a new currency, the *real,* and producing a balanced budget (in which income and spending are at least roughly equal). No one expected the Real Plan to succeed any

Brazilian President Fernando Henrique Cardoso and first lady Ruth Cordoso receive military honors during their arrival at the Superior Electoral Tribunal in Brasília, Brazil, December, 1998. The Tribunal honored Cardoso and his vice president, Marco Maciel, with a diploma for their reelection. It marked the first time in Brazilian history that a president received a reelection diploma.

better than the other economic schemes that had floundered during Brazil's modern history.

But it worked. Inflation fell to 21 percent by 1995. The poorest 50 percent of the population saw its share of income increased by 1.2 percent, or some $7.3 billion. The richest 20 percent of the population lost 2.3 percent, or $12 billion.

Cardoso was looked upon as a miracle man. He easily won the presidency in 1994. Losing badly was the Workers' Party candidate, Luiz Inácio Lula da Silva.

CHAPTER

3

Try and
Try Again

L ula was up against a formidable opponent in Fernando Henrique
Cardoso. Cardoso had made his record as the man who brought
inflation under control as President Itamar Franco's finance
minister. He also had impressive academic credentials. He held a
Ph.D. in sociology from the University of São Paulo and had studied
at the University of Paris. He, too, could testify to what it was like
to be arrested and interrogated by the military during the years of
the dictatorship.

His liberal views and his opposition to the military regime
led the generals to strip him of his political rights and his academic position at the University of São Paulo. But he continued to
speak out for democratic reforms and write articles that annoyed
the generals. He was arrested in the late 1960s, and the Center
for Analysis and Research, which he founded in São Paulo in

1968 as a social science think tank, was bombed by right-wing terrorists.

Cardoso was released from jail and left the country. He took teaching positions in the United States, France, and Chile. He returned to Brazil after the military dictatorship ended and became involved in politics. He was elected to the Senate in 1986 as a candidate of the Brazilian Social Democracy Party (PSDB), which he founded. He was reelected in 1988.

When Cardoso, born in 1931, became finance minister under Franco in 1993, he took a job nobody wanted because of the disastrous performance of the Brazilian economy. But he used it to get the economy back into shape, making his reputation. If Brazilians thought they needed somebody with a university education to run the country, they had that person in Cardoso.

In the first round of voting in 1994, Lula received only 27 percent of the presidential vote. He did poorly in the state of São Paulo, which was supposed to be a PT stronghold. One explanation was that the people were upset by the performance of the PT-sponsored mayor.

SOFT ON CRIME?

In addition, Lula was unfairly criticized as being "soft on crime." That accusation actually stemmed from the defeat of the PT's Benedita da Silva for mayor of Rio de Janeiro two years earlier. Benedita angered residents with her reaction to a beach riot led by teenagers from the slums. She explained the riot as the result of the social and economic despair of the people of the slums, where she had once lived.

But the people who suffered from the growing crime rate in the big cities did not want to hear sociology. They wanted the government to crack down on the thugs. When Lula said he agreed with Benedita's explanation, he was also branded as being soft on crime. Even lower-class voters, who might have sympathized with the causes of teenage angst in the slums, were turned off by the explanations. After all, they were the biggest victims of crime.

Finally, Lula and his supporters seemingly failed to realize how happy most people were with Cardoso's policies, which were leading to the sharp drop in inflation. Inflation was killing the people, and now it looked as if there was someone who knew how to deal with it. Lula's campaign could not come up with a good argument against what Cardoso had done for the economy.

Another factor was that the governments of Argentina and Chile were pursuing policies that were the opposite of what the PT favored, and were doing very well. Those countries had reduced state controls over the economy and had adopted free-market policies. If it worked for them, it would work for Brazil, the thinking went. However, it did not work long for Argentina, which plunged into a financial crisis in 2002 that rocked the whole hemisphere.

Cardoso needed a constitutional amendment to run for a second term in 1998. He felt he needed four more years to make many of his reform measures work. Congress passed the necessary amendment, and Cardoso was easily reelected. What possessed Lula to run against the popular president a second time is a mystery, but he did—and lost badly. Cardoso won with about 53 percent of the vote. Lula received about 32 percent.

Cardoso's popularity waned in his second term. For one thing, he had trouble getting his policies approved. His government was made up of a coalition of political parties, each of which had its own agenda. When politicians are exclusively out for themselves, it is the public that suffers.

DEALING WITH CORRUPTION

A financial crisis occurred when the governor of the key state of Minas Gerais, the former president Itamar Franco, threatened to default on the state's foreign debt. The value of the real fell in foreign markets and had to be bailed out by international monetary agencies.

President Fernando Cardoso, right, shows a decoration awarded to him by Portuguese President Jorge Sampaio, left, as Cardoso's wife, Ruth, looks on. Cardoso was in Lisbon to attend celebrations of the 500th annniversary of the transatlantic voyage of Portuguese navigator Pedro Alvares Cabral, the first European to reach what is now Brazil.

And Cardoso's fight against corruption, one of his campaign promises, did not go well. In one instance, Jader Barbalho, leader of the Brazilian Democratic Movement Party, part of Cardoso's coalition, and president of the Senate, was tainted by a financial scandal. Opponents accused his party of stealing from highway construction funds and draining the Amazon development agency. An audit showed that $830 million was missing.

Barbalho became quite rich during his political career, but an investigation of him could have implicated others and caused the scandal to spread. Cardoso did not win any points with the public when he tried, without success, to stop a congressional probe.

Cracking down on tax evasion by the rich was also another campaign pledge of Cardoso's, but to do so would have alienated key supporters among the elite.

Countries of the world are dependent on each other in many ways. It was once said that when the United States sneezes, the rest of the world catches cold. The same is true of Brazil to a lesser extent. Without foreign investment and international trade, a modern nation cannot survive.

A term, the "Brazil cost," has been used to express the concerns of the international community in the stability of Brazil. Brazil's record of "boom or bust" keeps international markets nervous. There were fears that the country would slip back into hyperinflation, build up a debt it could not pay, and face continued political upheavals, which have marked its up-and-down history. In other words, the "Brazil cost" involves how much it is going to cost a business to locate in Brazil or an investor to put money into the country, in the face of these fears.

In his book, *A History of Modern Brazil*, Colin M. MacLachlan cites the example of the Toyota Motor Corporation, the Japanese auto manufacturer. Toyota first invested in Brazil in 1952. Over the years, it opened assembly plants and parts factories, but it found that the unstable government was impossible to predict and deal with. Toyota couldn't make plans, a necessity for any company.

Government interference and political instability made Toyota overly cautious about how much it would invest in Brazil. Massive inflation caused the company to lose money.

During the Cardoso years, when the economy was more stable, Toyota found it could expand its operations and put more money into the country. It expanded its plant at Indaiatuba in São Paulo state in 2002 to increase production to 57,000 units. It also committed to increasing the installation of locally made parts for the new Corolla to 70 percent.

MONEY FLEES

How much Toyota would have invested in Brazil in the 50 years of its presence there had the country been stable is impossible to say. But it is obvious it would have been a lot. Money flees the country when investors lose confidence.

Brazil is very attractive to international investors because of the size of its market, but another concern is the poor distribution of wealth, with about a third of the population living below the poverty line. Who is going to buy the products made locally or imported?

There are also the issues of crime, aggravated by the drug trade, a lack of educational attainment, malnutrition, and other chronic health problems. (Brazil, though, has been highly praised for its AIDS programs.)

Jean Ziegler, the United Nations special representative for nutrition rights, toured the country in 2002 and was appalled by what he found. He said hunger in Brazil was "an act of [state] violence."

Widespread corruption in government and an inefficient bureaucracy have also made it tough to do business there (and expensive when bribes are demanded). Labor costs were high because the government provided job tenure (which can lead to keeping incompetent workers on the job), and social benefits. The estimated nonwage costs to businesses averaged 102 percent of the actual wage. Not many companies want to do business under these conditions.

A poll taken at the end of Cardoso's administration showed that voters had little confidence in the country's institutions. The military fared best with a 24.2 percent approval rating. The Chamber of Deputies received 3.4 percent and the Senate 2 percent.

Outgoing President Fernando Cardoso, during a press conference at the Planalto Palace government house in Brasília, October 28, 2002. Cardoso congratulated Lula da Silva on his recent election victory to succeed him as president in January 2003.

With Cardoso's term ending and the possibility of a left-wing candidate assuming the presidency, international bankers panicked again. The "Brazil cost" was back with a vengeance.

A CHANGE OF TONE

The International Monetary Fund, a United Nations agency that seeks to bring financial stabilization to the world, granted a $30 billion loan to Brazil in 2002. But, because of the political uncertainties, only $6 billion of it became immediately available. The rest was being held back to see what happened.

Lula faced an image problem. He had condemned the International Monetary Fund (a stand he later modified), and his party's calls for nationalizing key industries, restricting imports, and possibly refusing to pay international debts scared everyone. The party needed to modify its tone. Interestingly, a beautiful woman came to the rescue.

She was Marta Suplicy, an energetic, stylishly dressed, blond-haired woman who worked as a sex therapist. She had her own popular TV show in which she offered frank sexual advice. Then she switched to politics, and campaigned for mayor of São Paulo, Brazil's biggest city.

Her platform called for an end to corruption, and she vowed to attack the crime problem, homelessness, unemployment, and poverty. Despite a number of well-publicized romances, she won with 58 percent of the vote. She called her political philosophy "business-friendly socialism." She moved with equal ease among the poor, and the country's movers and shakers. Best of all, she was a member of the Workers' Party.

Her presence was reassuring to nervous voters and business executives alike. Her successes served to convince many voters that the PT was not just a shop-floor party of hairy-chested workers and wild-eyed radicals. If Marta Suplicy was a member, the PT could not be too scary.

And Lula himself spiffed up his image. He hired Duda Mendonca as his image consultant. Mendonca urged the candidate to show his naturally optimistic personality in public appearances and on television. He also made Lula get rid of his T-shirts and jeans and dress in conservative business suits by Armani. He got him cracking jokes on television.

Another strategist was José Dirceu de Oliveira e Silva, a federal deputy and president of the Workers' Party. He encouraged Lula to tone down the rhetoric that was frightening investors. Dirceu adopted slogans like "Lula Light," and "Little Lula Peace and Love." Although the changes infuriated the more radical elements of the PT, they worked to convince the business world that a Lula administration might not be so bad after all. Through Dirceu's efforts, the PT allied itself with the pro-business Liberal Party, bringing criticism from the more leftist members of the party.

Left-wing Workers' Party (PT) candidate Marta Suplicy gives a press conference in São Paulo, October 29, 2000. At the time, poll results showed Suplicy, former sex therapist and local television celebrity, ahead of the conservative candidate, former mayor and governor Paulo Maluf, in São Paulo's mayoral race. São Paulo is Brazil's financial capital and South America's largest city. Suplicy won the election.

"I am very upset with my party," said Heloisa Helena, a PT member in Alagoas state. "I gave up running for the governorship of Alagoas because I can't agree with the alliance. But it's better to have a broken heart than to sell your soul."

TELLING WASHINGTON

Dirceu made trips to meet with Wall Street bankers in New York and government leaders in Washington to tell them about the change—which he called "maturation"—in the probable new president of Brazil.

Dirceu had an interesting history himself. In 1969, the U.S. ambassador to Brazil, Charles Burke Elbrick, was kidnapped. The kidnappers demanded that 15 political prisoners of the military dictatorship be released. They were. One of them was José Dirceu.

He went to Cuba, where, it was said, he received guerrilla training. (Guerrillas are unofficial soldiers fighting for a cause.) In 1975, he sneaked back into Brazil with an assumed name, and got married. His wife never knew his true identity until a general amnesty, or pardon, was declared by the military government, and she saw him interviewed on television.

Cardoso, who could not run for another term, picked José Serra, a close friend who had been exiled with him during the military dictatorship, to succeed him. Serra, Cardoso's minister of health, shared Cardoso's political vision. Serra was a lackluster candidate. Another candidate, Ciro Gomez, the former governor of the state of Ceara and a Harvard University graduate, alienated the electorate with a couple of blunders. He called one member of the public a "donkey," and joked that his girlfriend, a popular soap opera star, was helping his campaign by sleeping with him.

Lula, the three-time loser, won 46.44 percent of the votes cast in the first round of balloting, and 61.4 percent against Serra in the second round, the largest percentage of any presidential candidate in Brazil. That figure edged out the record 58.8 percent that U.S. President Ronald Reagan won against Walter Mondale in 1984.

CARDOSO HONORED

As for Cardoso, he has gone on to a distinguished career as an elder statesman and educator. In 2003, he was awarded the J. William Fulbright Prize for International Understanding. The press release describing the honor stated, "During Dr. Cardoso's presidency from January 1995 to January 2003, he strengthened political institutions, increased economic stability and growth, and expanded educational opportunities for all Brazilians while promoting human rights and development.

"During his tenure, high school enrollments increased more than one third, and the number of students entering college doubled. Dr. Cardoso's emphasis on improving health care in poor rural areas resulted in a 25 percent decrease in infant mortality."

Dr. R. Fenton-May, the Fulbright Association president, said, "Dr. Cardoso has demonstrated an abiding concern about inequality and obstacles to human development. As an example, his dedication to creatively tackling social and health problems resulted in a 64 percent reduction in AIDS-related deaths in Brazil. His novel program has been recognized as a model for the rest of the world by the World Health Organization."

In 2003, Cardoso was appointed to a five-year term as professor-at-large at the Thomas J. Watson Jr. Institute for International Studies at Brown University. He has been a visiting professor at universities around the world, and has published books and articles on sociology, political science, and international relations.

He seemed none the worse for the wear and tear of trying to govern the remarkable nation that never ceases to amaze and frustrate the world.

4

From Colony to Republic

To understand the problems that Brazil and its leadership face today it is necessary to know something about the history of this amazing country.

When a fleet of Portuguese sailors under the command of Pedro Álvares Cabral first landed in 1500 on the coast of what would become Brazil, they thought they had found an island. They named it the Island of the True Cross (Vera Cruz). Later, when they arrived at what is now Guanabara Bay, they thought they had found a great river. They called it Rio de Janeiro, meaning the "River of January." Today, of course, Rio de Janeiro is the name of one of Brazil's world-famous cities, and is the former capital.

Cabral was actually on his way to India. The only way to sail to India from Portugal in those days was around the tip of Africa. That was where he was headed, but he veered so far to the west that he hit the South American coast. This was only a few years after Christopher Columbus landed in the Caribbean in 1492.

America was named in honor of Amerigo Vespucci, the Italian navigator who lived from 1454 to 1512, when he died of malaria. He worked for the Portuguese, and some years after Cabral's journey, he sailed along the coast of South America, charting the land and the rivers of what would be Brazil. The name *America* first appeared in reference to South America. The name *Brazil* came from the red dyewood tree, *pau brasil,* which was found to be plentiful in the new country. The settlers traded with the Indians for the wood, which produces a red dye.

MISSIONARIES ARRIVE

Brazil became a Portuguese colony, and Portuguese became the official language, unlike in its neighboring countries where Spanish is spoken. Gradually, the nation was expanded to reach today's boundaries. Much of the expansion was led by Catholic missionaries, who established missions deep into the hinterlands to convert the Indians to Catholicism. The Portuguese had to fight off the French in 1555, and then the Dutch, in 1654, to hold onto their possession.

Comparisons have been made between the histories of Brazil and the United States. Both started out as colonies of other great powers, Portugal for the Brazilians, and England for America. And both fought for their independence. For the United States, one war, the Revolution, won it independence. But for the Brazilians, many isolated outbreaks of rebellion had to occur before Portugal got the message.

In 1821, King João VI of Portugal appointed his son, Dom Pedro, as regent (a person appointed by a monarch to rule a country) of Brazil. On December 1, 1822, Dom Pedro proclaimed the independence of Brazil from Portugal in a ceremony on the plain of Ipiranga, near the city of São Paulo. He was crowned emperor of Brazil. He was called

Portraits of Dom Pedro II and his wife, Princess Isabella, as they appeared in the U.S. magazine *Harpers Weekly* in November 1889. Born in Rio de Janeiro December 2, 1825, and named Dom Pedro de Alcantara João Carlos Leopoldo Salvador Bibiano Franciso Xavier de Paula Leocadio Miguel Gabriel Rafael Gonzaga de Bragança e Borbón by his ruling parents, the young boy was proclaimed emperor on April 14, 1841, after his father and stepmother left the country. An advocate of education and learning, Dom Pedro once said that if he hadn't been emperor, he would have been a schoolteacher.

Pedro I. The United States was the first country to recognize the new nation.

Brazil's first Constitution was approved in 1824. The United States was far ahead of Brazil in adopting a Constitution, having done so in 1787. And unlike Brazil, the United States never went through a period as an empire.

Pedro I had many problems ruling this vast country. For one thing, it lost the territory that would become Uruguay after a war with Argentina in the mid-1820s. There were pressures to abolish the slave trade, which the farmers, like Southern planters in the United States, thought they could not survive without. Pedro could not get along with the legislature and was preoccupied with affairs in Portugal. Finally, he just quit. He sailed back to Portugal in 1831, leaving his 5-year-old son as regent.

THE BOY EMPEROR

Chaos resulted. No longer was anyone in charge. Pedro II was too young to rule. Theoretically, he could not take over until he was 18. A couple of regents tried to govern, but failed. The country was in serious trouble and needed a strong leader.

Finally, the nation decided that Pedro II had to become the ruler, young as he was. So, on July 23, 1840, the General Assembly (the lawmaking body) voted to let Pedro II become emperor. He was sworn in that afternoon. He was 14.

Pedro II was not ready to rule. He had lost his parents at an early age and was raised by court attendants. He had a high-pitched voice and a love of sweets that quickly made him pudgy. But gradually he rose to the occasion. Pedro II grew a beard that made him look more mature, and he married and had children, easing his problems.

The marriage to Thereza Christina, the daughter of King Francis I of Naples, almost did not happen. Since the marriage was an arranged one, the couple did not see each other until she arrived in Brazil for the wedding. When the 18-year-old Pedro climbed aboard the ship that brought his bride to him in Guanabara Bay, he almost sent her back. As one writer described Thereza, she was "short, stocky, sallow of skin, coarse-featured, and walked with a limp." Pedro, however, was too much of a gentleman to reject his intended bride and they were married. He learned to love her, and she remained with him throughout his long reign. She became popular with the Brazilian people for her kindness and motherly manner. She died of a heart attack in 1889, a month after Pedro gave up the throne.

Pedro also became popular with the people. He was polite, humble, and charming. He didn't care for ceremony and was often criticized for not assuming the trappings of a monarch. His palaces were not as grand as the homes of many of the nation's rich families.

When the famous French actress Sarah Bernhardt, who had hobnobbed with European royalty, performed in Rio, she was shocked by Pedro's demeanor. She was particularly upset when he arrived at one of her performances in a carriage drawn by mules. When Pedro was in England to meet Queen Victoria, she was offended that he showed up at a formal ball in a black frock coat.

POPULAR VISITOR

Whether it was intentional or not, Pedro had adopted some of the homey characteristics of Abraham Lincoln, who was president of the United States (1861–1865) during part of Pedro's reign. Lincoln never lost much of his backwoods character, and also didn't care for ceremony and putting on airs. His famous Gettysburg Address was roundly criticized at the time as being too short, and he was regularly attacked in the press as an embarrassment to the country.

When Pedro II traveled to the United States in 1876, the year of America's centennial (100-year) celebration, he caused a sensation. His visit to New Orleans had people cheering him in the streets, "Long live the Emperor!" This bearded, portly gentleman charmed everyone he met.

One of his interests was how Southern plantation owners had adjusted to the abolition of slavery in America. Slavery was still a strong institution in Brazil at that time. He was told that free labor proved even more productive than slave labor, although it was obvious that not everyone in the South felt that way.

Back home, Dom Pedro enjoyed nothing better than visiting schools. Improving education was one of his pet projects. He once said that if he weren't emperor he would have liked to have been a school teacher.

Although the 49-year rule of Pedro II was marked by progress in many fields, the period was marred by a long and bloody war with Paraguay, from 1864 to 1870. Brazil, Argentina and Uruguay fought Paraguay, which had an efficient and well-trained military under the dictator Francisco Solano López. The conflict was called the War of the Triple Alliance, and was the bloodiest war in South American history.

The three allies finally succeeded in overthrowing Lopez, but at enormous cost. The war cost more than $300 million and required 200,000 men to be mobilized. About 50,000 Brazilians died or were wounded in the conflict, which left the country in debt and caused inflation. The war also created a powerful military that would influence and often control Brazil for the rest of its history.

Brazil celebrated the victory over Paraguay on January 5, 1869. But Lopez proved to be a stubborn enemy. He conducted a guerrilla campaign against the allies for about a year. Finally, Brazilian soldiers defeated his last remaining forces and killed him.

WORRIED PLANTERS

The war had the unexpected effect of delaying the abolition of slavery. The wealthy farmers who owned slaves were always worried about a slave rebellion. They were well aware of how a slave uprising led by Toussaint L'Ouverture on the island of Santo Dominique in the Caribbean overthrew the French in 1801 and created the nation of Haiti. The farmers were afraid this would happen in Brazil, and, with the army fighting Paraguay, there was no available force to put down such a rebellion.

Brazil's agriculture at that time was the most important element of its economy. Industrialization had not yet occurred. The slaves worked on large plantations, similar to those in the American South. Cotton, coffee, and sugar were the main crops, and there was a big export trade. The United States was one of Brazil's major customers.

Although Brazil formally abolished the slave trade in 1831 under pressure from Great Britain, then a "superpower" in the world, the trade continued for another 20 years. In 1871, what was called the "Law of the Free Womb" was adopted. It declared that all children born to slaves were free. This did not satisfy the abolitionists (those who wanted to abolish, or end, slavery). They had become a strong voice in Brazil.

One of the movement's leaders was Antonio Bento, who rivaled the United States's John Brown for his fierce opposition to slavery. Bento was mentally unbalanced (as most historians believe John Brown was). He was obsessed by religion and considered slavery evil. He set out to terrify the slaveholders. He would stride around in a long black cape and tall black hat, confronting slave owners and their supporters with burning eyes and a loud voice. Bento ran an Underground Railroad to transport and hide runaway slaves, reminiscent of the same system adopted by abolitionists in the United States. He collected and displayed torture implements that he claimed were used by slave masters to keep their slaves in line. Bento brought many people to his cause, but he was never hanged, as John Brown was in 1859 after his bloody takeover of the Army arsenal at Harpers Ferry in West Virginia.

A less violent abolitionist was a lawyer named Joaquim Nabuco de Araujo, who wrote an important book about aboli-tion in 1883. The states of Ceara and Amazonas freed their slaves in 1884, and in 1885 all slaves over age 60 were declared free. On May 13, 1888, slavery was finally abolished. More than 700,000 slaves were freed.

About that time, many forward-looking leaders began to think of replacing the monarchy with a republican form of government. In a republic, the people rule through their elected representatives. The Republican Party was created in 1870, and gradually became a potent force in Brazilian politics. (It had no relation to the Republican Party in the United States.)

THE GROWING COUNTRY

Meanwhile, Brazil was developing rapidly. The population grew from 4 million to 14 million during the reign of Pedro II. There was a fourteen-fold increase in public revenues (from taxes, fees, and other levies), and a ten-fold increase in the value of the products of the empire.

By 1889, railroad mileage reached 5,000 miles (8,047 km). The first railroad was built in Brazil in 1854. After 1840, coffee became the nation's biggest product. By 1908, coffee accounted for 53 percent of the country's exports. And Brazilian coffee was popular all over the world.

The factors that brought an end to the empire are many and controversial. For one thing, many people blamed the empire form of government for the prolonged war against Paraguay. But a general consensus was building that a monarchy was no longer the way to govern a country that was plunging headfirst into the future. The monarchy was rooted in the past, while many thought that a republic would better point the country toward the modernization everyone was counting on to improve life.

The pressures mounted and the military finally forced Pedro to abdicate. On November 15, 1889, he sailed for Europe, and Brazil entered into a new phase of its history. Dom Pedro died of pneumonia in a hotel room in Paris on December 5, 1891.

Provincial railroads in Brazil, circa 1902. The first Brazilian railway, build in 1854, was a little under 9 miles long. By the 1870s, railways leading inland from Rio de Janeiro had contributed to the growth of many smaller cities.

The republic was established by Marshal Deodoro da Fonseca, who ran the country as provisional president after the emperor left. He put forth a new Constitution that went into effect on February 24, 1891. The Congress elected him president that year.

THE PRESIDENT QUITS

Fonseca was the first president of Brazil. But he spent most of his time in office battling with the Congress, and finally dissolved it and ruled by decree. This move upset elements of the Army and Navy, and the Navy threatened to bomb Rio. It actually did fire one cannon shot, which knocked over a church steeple.

Fonseca got the message loud and clear. He resigned and turned the presidency over to the vice president, Marshal Floriano Peixoto. Fonseca died the following year. Peixoto ruled almost like a dictator. He was a man of little schooling who distrusted anyone who was better educated and more socially prominent than he. But he was credited with bringing a certain degree of peace to Brazil after putting down insurrections by the military and those who wanted the return of the emperor.

In 1894, Peixoto turned over the presidency to Prudente de Morais, who had been the first republican governor of São Paulo. Morais became the nation's first civilian president on November 23, 1894.

The industrialization of Brazil could be said to have started with Irineu Evangelista de Sousa (1813–1889). He was only 13 when he started working for a British importing firm in Brazil. It took him just seven years to become a partner in the firm, and he eventually became manager.

When he visited England in the 1840s, he was impressed at how far the British had progressed into the Industrial Revolution. He brought back to Brazil the ideas that industrialization and banking were the way to go. The government of Pedro II lent money to him and other visionaries to further their activities. In 1850, Evangelista established an iron works that produced pipes to drain the swamps around Rio. It also built ships and employed about 300 workers. After the first railroad was built, he engaged in many railroad projects.

Evangelista was an early abolitionist who felt that free labor would contribute to industrialization. Although he ran into financial difficulties and built up a debt that he was still paying off at his death, he is credited with advancing the modernization of Brazil with his foresight and enterprise.

Another of Evangelista's businesses was a steamship line that traveled the mighty Amazon River. Steam came to Brazil as early as 1819, but coastal shipping was still dependent on sail. In 1843, a steamship called *Guapiassu* made the trip up the Amazon from Belem on the coast to Manaus, a distance of almost 1,000 miles (1,609 km), and returned within 15 days. By sail, the trip had taken three to four months. The country was stunned.

TRAINING THE POOR

An important step in modernizing labor came with the creation of the Apprentice Sailor School in 1840. The school trained orphans and street children in the skills of shipbuilding and seamanship. Similar technical schools sprang up, and Brazil was on its way to producing skilled workers to replace the foreign technicians who were previously brought into the country to work in the new industries.

The Constitution of 1891 did away with the requirement that only property owners could vote. However, it still prevented illiterates (people who cannot read or write) and women from voting. (Women didn't get the vote until 1936.)

Coffee continued to dominate the export trade and the next few presidents were called the "coffee presidents" because of the growers' strong influence on the government. Only gradually did coffee's influence wane as other areas of the globe began producing the product. Also, overproduction led to

Spreading coffee beans, circa 1940. Coffee once accounted for more than 50 percent of Brazil's agricultural exports; that number has dropped drastically in recent years.

decreases in prices that often made coffee no longer economically feasible to produce. Coffee exports dropped to 5 percent of Brazil's total exports in the early twenty-first century.

Brazil was entering the modern era as the nineteenth century came to a close. What lay ahead was the destruction of much of the country's natural beauty, as well as pollution, poverty, child labor, drug gangs, military dictatorship, a murder rate that stunned the world, and myriad other problems of unchecked and unregulated growth.

The rich kept getting richer, and the poor kept getting poorer.

5

A Republic's Growing Pains

T he republic was doomed. There were many reasons for the discontent that finally killed it and led to a military dictatorship. Brazil was a nation long ruled by the elite. In the early days, the elite was made up of planters, who grew coffee, sugar, and cotton and sent those products all over the world. But as industrialization began, it brought new demands by workers to get a bigger slice of the economic pie. Unions won legal recognition in 1907.

The people were tired of the "coffee presidents." For years, the presidency was passed back and forth between political leaders from São Paulo and Minas Gerais, the two most powerful states, powerful because of coffee.

Throughout Brazil's early history, not much of a middle-class existed. The population was basically divided between the haves and the have-nots—the rich and the poor. But with industrialization and the weakening of the agricultural elite, a restless middle class was growing.

A further division existed between the people of the countryside, the huge expanse of backlands, as they were called, and the people who lived in the cities along the coast. They had practically nothing in common. Some people referred to this division as the "two Brazils."

And the military began to assert itself. For years after the republic was founded, the military had pretty much kept its hands off the government. But as discontent over the republic deepened, the military began to take on a more prominent role.

There was one peculiar military uprising in 1904 that serves as an illustration of the Brazilian character. Dr. Oswaldo Cruz was named director of the Federal Department of Health. His job was to do away with the dangerous illnesses that were killing people in the cities, like yellow fever, smallpox, and the plague. He started new prevention programs, including the eradication of rats and mosquitoes, which carried disease. But he ran into trouble when he tried to impose mandatory smallpox vaccination on people.

People objected to forced vaccination, no matter how good it might be for them. They felt it violated their freedom of choice. Rioting occurred in the streets. Cadets from the military academy in Rio de Janeiro joined street rioters to oppose the forced vaccinations. So the government backed off. As a result, a smallpox plague in 1908 killed 9,000 people.

THE LIEUTENANTS

But a more serious military uprising occurred in 1924. One of its leaders was a remarkable man named Luiz Carlos Prestes, who was a lieutenant at the time. He was joined by other young officers, mostly fellow lieutenants. The action became known as the revolt of the *tenentes*—lieutenants.

They launched a rebellion in Rio de Janeiro that was easily quashed by government troops. Prestes was suffering from typhoid fever and did not participate in the actual revolt, so the government did not identify him with the rebellion.

Later, he was involved in another revolt, this time in São Paulo, that was more successful. The rebels held onto the city for three weeks before being overtaken by government troops.

By that time, Prestes was a captain and he began what has come down in Brazilian history as an amazing adventure. It began when he led a column of troops to the interior of the state of São Paulo, where it was joined by rebels from that city. From there, some 1,500 soldiers under his command started out on a two-and-a-half-year march through 13 states. His goal was to encourage others to join him for a final confrontation with the government.

To his disgust, however, he found that most Brazilians in the backlands were afraid of revolutionary change and refused to join what became known as the "Prestes Column." Convinced by the rich landowners whom they worked for that Prestes and his men were their enemies, some workers actually attacked the column, resulting in several bloody clashes.

But Prestes became a national hero. He was called the "Cavalier of Hope." People eagerly kept up with the progress of his long march through newspaper accounts. Prestes was a small man, not very imposing, but he had a brilliant mind and the ability to convince others of the worthiness of his cause.

Eventually, though, his crusade ran out of steam. His column, down to about 620 men, crossed into Bolivia and gave up its campaign in 1927. A month later, about 66 members crossed into Paraguay.

COMMUNIST INFLUENCE

Prestes's program for change included honest elections; social legislation to make life better for the poor; an end to government corruption, which was nearly a way of life in Brazil; and an end to excessive taxes and political persecution of government opponents.

The Communist Party, which had become an influential force in the country, took to Prestes. Leaders saw in him a way to gain control of the government for the party, which was then run from Moscow.

Many of the men who had marched with Prestes returned to Brazil and joined the revolution that brought an end to the republic. Not Prestes, however. He joined the Communist Party and, with his mother and siblings, moved to Moscow. He worked there as an engineer for a few years and became a member of the executive committee of the Comintern (the international organization of Communist parties directed from Moscow).

The Communists by then were getting cocky. They thought they could stage a successful revolution in Brazil, and the leaders ordered Prestes to go back in 1935 and lead it. He was accompanied on the trip home by a fascinating woman named Olga Benario. She was a German Jew, young, pretty and fluent in four languages, although she could not speak Portuguese. She was also an excellent shot, a pilot, and a parachutist. On the trip, the two fell in love.

But their love affair, and the revolution they were supposed to lead, were both doomed. Troops loyal to the government of President Getúlio Vargas easily crushed the Communist uprising. Prestes was sentenced to 47 years in prison, and Olga was deported to Germany. She died in a Nazi concentration camp.

In 1945, at the end of World War II, Prestes was released from prison. Many still regarded him as a hero, and they felt sorry for the loss of his beloved Olga. Prestes lived underground for 10 years, finally resurfacing when restrictions on the Communist Party were temporarily lifted. But he had to go underground again when the new military government clamped down on Communists.

He returned to Moscow with a new wife, and they had eight children. Eventually, even the Communists grew tired of him, and he was kicked out of the party in 1984. Although he continued to speak out on Brazilian issues, few people paid much attention any more to the onetime Cavalier of Hope. He died of a heart attack on March 7, 1990, at age 92.

RUBBER BARONS

Before 1929, Brazil was doing well economically. The prosperity was mostly the result of the great worldwide demand for Brazilian products, most notably coffee and rubber. The United States, England, and Germany were Brazil's major customers.

Rubber trees grow in abundance in northern Brazil. In ancient times, Indians used the latex drawn from rubber trees to waterproof their canoes. Early colonialists made boots from rubber. But it wasn't until 1840 that Charles Goodyear, the American founder of the Goodyear Tire and Rubber Company, discovered how to keep rubber from becoming sticky in heat and brittle in cold. The process was called *vulcanization,* and it revolutionized the use of rubber.

Rubber quickly found many uses in industry, and, eventually, in the manufacture of tires, for bicycles and ultimately automobiles. Although rubber was produced elsewhere in the world, the latex from Brazilian trees was thought to be the best.

People became rich producing rubber. Towns along the Amazon River where the rubber trees grew became bustling cities. One of them, Manaus, a river port nearly 1,000 miles (1,609 km) from the ocean, was transformed almost overnight from a village of jungle huts to a modern city that even had its own opera house. Rubber barons were so rich that they sent their laundry to Paris.

Thousands of laborers were needed to tap the rubber trees. To get to the trees, they had to enter lands occupied by the Indians, and bloody fighting resulted. The rubber barons were ruthless. They organized the massacre of 40,000 Indians who dared to interfere with their production.

The man credited with destroying the Brazilian rubber trade was Henry Wickham. He was an Englishman who managed

Collecting latex from a rubber tree. Before 1929, and especially with the advent of the automobile in Brazil in 1915, Brazil's exportation of rubber provided prosperity for the country. The Brazilian rubber trade collapsed in 1929, however when a shipload of rubber tree seeds were smuggled out of the country and planted in Asia. Eventually, competition from Asia drastically reduced importers' demands for the Brazilian variety, which until then had been superior to rubber produced anywhere else in the world.

to smuggle a shipload of rubber seeds to England aboard the SS *Amazonas.* The seeds were sent to Ceylon, where they were planted and were soon producing Brazilian latex. Ceylon, an island in the Indian Ocean, is now known as Sri Lanka. Wickham was called the "Executioner of Amazonas."

TERRIBLE ROADS

The Ford Motor Company established a subsidiary in Brazil in 1919. An assembly plant produced the company's famous Model T. A Model T assembled in Brazil was a big attraction at an automobile exhibition held in São Paulo's Palace of Industry in 1925.

The problem with introducing automobiles to Brazil was that the roads were terrible. However, an adventurer named Colonel Candido Mariano da Silva Rondon drove a Ford into the backlands over roads that were little more than trails. He erected telegraph poles as he went.

By 1925, Ford had sold 24,000 cars in Brazil. General Motors arrived in 1925 and by 1928, sold 50,000 cars. GM placed its cars on trains and rode around the countryside, selling its products to a middle class that was flattered by a sales pitch aimed at them.

But, like every other economic boom that Brazil had experienced through its history, a bust was inevitable. The rubber trade collapsed, as competition from rubber plantations in Asia ended Brazil's monopoly.

The most crushing blow, though, was the worldwide Depression that began in 1929 in the United States. Suddenly, Brazil's major customers could no longer afford its products. To make matters worse, the United States, trying to save banks that were rapidly going out of business, raised the interest rates on Brazil's debts. So Brazil had to pay more on its debts while its income was reduced.

The situation was critical, and the president at the time, Washington Luís Pereira de Sousa, made it even more critical.

He alienated the coffee planters, still a powerful group, by doing away with the government's policy of buying up the coffee surplus to keep the price up.

FATHER OF THE POOR

For a time, Getúlio Vargas seemed to be the savior of the country. But his story ended in failure and tragedy. In the beginning, though, the man who called himself the "Father of the Poor" delivered on his promises.

He brought in a new generation of young, energetic administrators who set about to transform the economy and the political system. He nationalized the oil, electricity, and steel industries. That means he took them out of private ownership and place them under government control. Vargas also set up a health and social welfare system that made him extremely popular among the working class during his terms in office— and even after his death.

But Vargas alienated many others. He scrapped the old Constitution that established the republic. He became a dictator, did away with Congress, replaced the governors of all but one state with his own people, locked up anybody who didn't agree with him, fought the trade unions, and outlawed the Communist Party. He called his regime the "Estado Novo," the New State.

One writer described Vargas as "a small man obsessed with power. Relentless yet good-natured, crafty yet bland . . . Vargas viewed the presidency as a vehicle for authoritative rule, but not personal aggrandizement."

In other words, he did what he felt he had to for the country, without much thought of personal glory.

Under Vargas's leadership, Brazil declared war on the Axis powers—Germany, Italy, and Japan—during World War II. The Vargas administration had become outraged at having its merchant ships sunk by German submarines using bases in Argentina and Chile.

Brazil had declared war on Germany during World War I, but its troops never saw combat. World War II was different. The country sent the Brazilian Expeditionary Force to Italy to join the Allies in the bitter Italian Campaign. The force eventually totaled 25,300 men. The troops fought bravely, and suffered many casualties. Brazilian troops also fought in Southern France and participated in the Normandy invasion.

Paradoxically, Brazil's participation in World War II helped bring Vargas down. After the war, the Army gained more prestige and influence. Some of those who fought began to realize that they had been battling against dictatorships only to return home to a dictatorship.

6

From a Dictatorship to a Dictatorship

Getúlio Vargas was born in 1883 in the state of Rio Grande do Sul, the southernmost state of Brazil. It was a land of cattle and gauchos (cowboys). The people were tough and independent, similar to the cattle-raising Westerners in the United States.

His family was prosperous and had political connections, which no doubt gave Getúlio an early interest in politics. The political machine in Rio Grande do Sul was then run by Antonio Augusto Borges de Medeiros. Vargas became part of that organization and took a series of governmental positions. He served in the State Assembly and later was a congressman in the Brazilian Legislature. He also served in the Army.

When Washington Luís Pereira won the Brazilian presidency in 1926, he named Vargas finance minister. It was a kind of payoff for the support of the Borges de Medeiros machine in his election.

The job gave Vargas valuable experience with national politics and finance. He returned to Rio Grande do Sul and was elected governor in 1928.

By 1930, Vargas was being touted as a presidential candidate. But Pereira angered politicians by deviating from the unwritten rule at the time that the presidency had to alternate between São Paulo state and Minas Gerais state. Since Pereira was from São Paulo, he should have selected someone from Minas Gerais as his successor. Instead, he chose Júlio Prestes (no relation to the Cavalier of Hope), who also was from São Paulo.

Leaders of Brazil's southern states were outraged when the government announced that Prestes won the election in 1930. The assassination of an official from Vargas's party, the Liberal Alliance, was the last straw. The southern states sent an army, with Vargas as one of its leaders, to Rio de Janeiro.

In his diary, Vargas wrote on October 3, 1930, that it was the day of revolution.

"All the arrangements made," he wrote, "all the calls made. It certainly will be today at 5 P.M. . . . I had a quiet lunch with my family and went for a ping-pong match with my wife as I usually do every day . . . Four-thirty. The time comes. I feel peaceful in spirit, as someone who plays a decisive move because he couldn't find another honorable solution. . . .

"The movement has started. A live volley of rifle shots and machine guns. . . ."

The Army of Brazil, as it called itself, deposed Pereira to keep him from turning the presidency over to Prestes. A provisional government was established with Vargas as its leader.

In 1933, Vargas was elected to a four-year term as president of Brazil. He formed a new Constitution, which became effective in 1934. The Communists, who thought this was a chance to take over the government, launched the revolution led by Luís Carlos Prestes, the Cavalier of Hope. There were many casualties, and a frightened public did not object when

Vargas used the revolt as an excuse to declare martial law, abolish Congress, and make himself dictator.

PROMISES, PROMISES

Vargas—the "Father of the Poor"—was a stubborn man. When his term was due to end in 1937, he carried out a *coup d'etat*, and created the Estado Novo, the New State, with a new Constitution that kept him on as president. *Coup d'etat* is a French term meaning the overthrow of a government either by force or an unconstitutional action. Vargas used no force. No blood was spilled, but he stubbornly held onto the presidency under the new government he had established.

Once again, the time came for him to leave office in 1943, but he held on, using the excuse that World War II had created an emergency situation. He promised new elections soon. He repeated that vow in 1944, but no elections were scheduled.

With the war over, the military decided Vargas had to go. A group of officers confronted him in October 1945 and gave him an ultimatum—get out or they would throw him out. Vargas declared that he would resist. He had weapons in the presidential palace, and he would use them to fight anyone trying to remove him from office.

The military leaders had no intention of engaging in a blazing gun battle with the president and his supporters. Instead, they said they would cut off water and electricity to the palace and wait for him to surrender.

It didn't look as if Vargas was going to go down shooting. "I would prefer that you all attack me and my death remain as a protest against this violence," he announced. "But as this is to be a bloodless *coup d'etat,* I shall not be a cause of disturbance."

So Vargas left office and supported General Eurico Gaspar Dutra as his successor. Dutra won the election in December 1945, and a new Constitution was created in September 1946. One of its purposes was to try to prevent another dictatorship. Vargas, though, was not finished with politics. He was elected to the Senate and was relatively quiet for four years. But his popularity remained high, and he was elected president again in 1950.

It was not a good time for the once-mighty dictator. High inflation and other economic problems plagued the country. Dwight D. Eisenhower, who was elected U.S. president in 1952, cut off economic aid that had been provided by the Roosevelt and Truman administrations. Brazil was no longer needed as an ally now that the war was over.

In addition, Vargas's physical and mental condition deteriorated. In 1953, he fell and broke an arm and a leg. He suffered from insomnia and depression. His popularity slipped, and he was barraged by constant criticism.

MORE CORRUPTION

One of his major critics was a newspaper owner named Carlos Lacerda. In 1954, someone tried to kill Lacerda, but succeeded only in killing his bodyguard. There was outrage in the country. Everyone thought Vargas was behind the shooting. As it turned out, an overeager supporter of Vargas's had carried out the shooting in a misguided attempt to do the president a favor. But an investigation into the attack led to the discovery of widespread corruption in the Vargas administration. Vargas himself was not involved, but it was his responsibility to keep his administration clean.

Finally, the military again had to take action. Officers confronted Vargas once more, this time on the night of August 24, 1954. When he was handed the new ultimatum, he sat down and wrote a note. He then went to his bedroom and shot himself in the heart.

The lengthy note was read to the people over the radio. It said in part:

"There is nothing more I can give you except my blood. . . . I choose this means of being always with you. When they humiliate you, you will feel my soul suffering at your side.

When hunger knocks at your door, you will feel in your breast the energy to struggle for yourselves and your children. When you are scorned, my memory will give you the strength to react. My sacrifice will keep you united, and my name will be your battle standard.

"Each drop of my blood will be an immortal flame in your conscience and will uphold the sacred will to resist."

These heartfelt words moved the populace. The day of his death became a day of national remembrance observed by newspapers and magazines with long articles about what a great leader he had been.

Vice President João Café Filho served out Vargas's term. On October 3, 1955, Juscelino Kubitschek de Oliveira was elected president, and João Goulart won the separate election as vice president. But like much of Brazilian politics, it wasn't that easy.

Before the two could be inaugurated, Café Filho had a mild heart attack and turned the presidency over to Carlos Luz, speaker of the Chamber of Deputies, as the Constitution provided. Luz announced that he would replace Marshal Teixeira Lott to resolve a dispute between the war minister and the administration.

Kubitschek's supporters saw this move as an attempt to prevent their man from taking office. On November 11, 1955, Teixeira Lott and Marshal Odilio Denys, commander of army troops in Rio de Janeiro, staged what would have been a countercoup if a coup had taken place. Luz was kicked out of office, and Kubitschek and Goulart took over peacefully.

Kubitschek was considered an heir to the Vargas regime. But he embarked on a program of modernization for Brazil, building highways and power projects, and expanding iron, steel, petroleum, and coal production with government assistance. His campaign slogan was. "Fifty years of progress in five."

President Juscelino Kubitschek, holding a press conference for the inauguration of Brasília, the new Brazilian capital, in April 1960. One of Kubitschek's campaign promises was that if he were elected, he would move the capital to Brasília, inland and 580 miles northwest of the old capital, Rio de Janeiro.

OPTIMISM REIGNS

Kubitschek was an optimistic man. His enthusiasm for Brazil's future was contagious. He encouraged industrial expansion, and new industries increased by 33 percent and employed 2 million people.

During his presidency, Brazil won soccer's World Cup in Sweden in 1958, with the great Pelé as the star. A Brazilian woman, Maria Bueno, became an international tennis celebrity when she won at Wimbledon in 1959 and 1960. Jet travel between Rio and New York began. The new power projects boosted hydroelectric power from three million to five million kilowatts, and better transmission lines took the energy to the new industries.

When General Motors built a plant between São Paulo and Rio, Kubitschek donned a fire-resistant suit and poured molten steel into a motor block. The people loved it.

A new musical beat, the bossa nova, a mixture of American jazz and Brazilian samba, swept the country. People were feeling good about themselves and their country.

But Kubitschek's major claim to fame might be the building of Brasília as the nation's new capital. The site is 580 miles (933 km) northwest of the old capital of Rio de Janeiro. In other words, in the middle of nowhere.

Kubitschek, though, had a plan. His idea was to call more attention to the interior of the country and encourage settlements there and exploitation of its natural resources. A bright, shining, modern city was built, and on April 21, 1960, it was dedicated as the nation's capital. Residents of Rio were upset, but the rest of Brazil approved of the new city.

Unfortunately, Kubitschek's development programs were overly ambitious. He spent money like water. High inflation resulted, and an enormous foreign debt built up. And, as usual, the great mass of the population benefited little from the expansion.

In other words, the rich continued to get richer and the poor and the middle class either got poorer, or didn't budge.

It was a familiar story for Brazil.

HOW TO FAKE IT

Corruption continued unabated. One scandal over the years involved what was called *grilagem*, which refers to the practice

Neon signs reflected in the water of Brasília, the preplanned capital of Brazil. In 1987, UNESCO named Brasília part of the world heritage. The city's population elected its first government officials in October 1990.

of turning over millions of acres of public land to favored private parties. To do so, fake documents were used.

Grilagem means "cricketing." To make the phony documents look as old as they were supposed to be, a cricket was placed in the box with the papers. Over time, its excrement would make the documents appear to be stained with age.

When Kubitschek left the presidency, the country was broke, in debt, and emotionally exhausted.

By 1960, the country was back to its customary economic mess. Janio Quadros, considered a maverick politician, was elected president. João Goulart, who was also considered an heir to the Vargas regime, was reelected vice president.

Quadros, who had been governor of São Paulo state, almost immediately ran into problems. He did not get along with Congress, where many people who had been loyal to Vargas remained, and he was prevented from enacting very many reforms or actions to control inflation.

In foreign affairs, he tried to move the country away from dependence on the United States. He established relations with the Soviet Union, and supported Fidel Castro's Communist regime in Cuba.

Quadros was a failure as a president, and in his personal habits. He was unkempt, his clothes looked like he had slept in them, his shoes were scuffed, and his uncombed hair hung in his eyes. He looked like Groucho Marx with his bushy mustache and shock of black hair. Visitors usually found him sitting behind his desk with his feet propped up. He did weird things, like trying to ban bikinis on Copacabana Beach. He liked to retire to a private screening room to watch movies with a bottle of Scotch whiskey.

On August 25, 1961, Quadros abruptly resigned. He had been in office only seven months. He claimed "terrible forces" were against him. He left Brazil in a shambles.

His action caused a crisis, especially since Vice President Goulart was in China. The Congress installed Pascoal Ranieri Mazzilli, speaker of the Chamber of Deputies, as president. When Goulart returned home, he was surprised by what had gone on behind his back. He declared that he was the real president. The military and other powerful forces thought he was too radical for the job. Civil war seemed imminent. But at the last moment, a compromise was reached. The country would be converted to a parliamentary form of government. Goulart would be president, but he would only be a figurehead. The power would be in the hands of a prime minister, Tancredo Neves, who would later be elected president.

The parliamentary form of government is the system in effect in Great Britain and other Western countries, where it has worked for centuries. But in Brazil, it was another story.

EXPERIMENT ENDS

The government decided to ask the electorate if it wanted to continue with the parliamentary form or support Goulart as the sole head of state. The vote gave Goulart full presidential powers, and that ended the parliamentary experiment. However, Goulart was unable to help the economy. In early 1964, inflation reached 100 percent. He worried military leaders by surrounding himself with left-wing advisers.

Goulart was also a rather pitiful character. There were rumors that his wife was having an affair. One of his legs was shorter than the other, causing him to limp and leading to cruel jokes.

He was nicknamed "Jango." He was a friend of Argentina's dictator, Juan Peron, and critics said he intended to impose a Peron-type rule on Brazil. He seemed a little too cozy with Communists and radical union leaders, whose political backing he needed. In other words, he had a knack for alienating people on the left and the right. Goulart was a protégé of Getúlio Vargas, and anti-Vargas forces attacked him.

His downfall may have started on March 13, 1964, when he staged an ill-advised rally in Rio de Janeiro in which he announced a series of decrees that would nationalize oil refineries and take over large amounts of undeveloped land. (Fidel Castro alienated the United States when he nationalized American oil refineries in Cuba after taking over in 1959.)

What was considered the "last straw" for Jango occurred at the end of the month when he permitted his minister of the Navy to grant amnesty to a group of sailors who had gone on strike to create a union of enlisted men. A union of military people! The generals were not about to tolerate any such thing.

A group of military leaders and other enemies of Goulart had been plotting to get rid of him for some time. Left-wingers threatened violence if the army tried to take over the country. Troops and tanks rolled into the major cities. Tear gas filled the air. But there were no disturbances. The army established control of the country within 48 hours. On April 2, 1964, Goulart fled to Uruguay. Once again, Ranieri Mazzilli was installed as temporary president.

Brazil's long dark night of military dictatorships began. Within the first six months, there were mass arrests of people considered enemies of the state. Union and government officials—including past presidents Goulart, Quadros, and Kubitschek—were deprived of political rights.

Kubitschek left Brazil and spent the years of the military dictatorship in the United States and Europe. He returned to Brazil in 1976, but was killed in a car crash.

Under the dictatorships, there would be no more opposition political parties. Unions were deprived of power. Newspapers were censored. People who opposed the regime were made to "disappear." Enemies were arrested and tortured. Some died under torture.

ANOTHER CONSTITUTION

On April 11, 1964, the Congress elected Humberto de Alencas Castelo Branco president. A new Constitution was enacted in 1967. It confirmed what had already been done, giving most power to the central government. It also established the policy of using military courts to judge people accused of threatening national security.

Under Branco, a rigged two-party system was installed, in an attempt to give the military regime more legitimacy. One party was the pro-government National Renewal Alliance. The other, an opposition party, was called the Brazilian Democratic Movement. However, when Movement candidates won the governorships of the key states of Guanabara and Minas

Gerais, the national government effectively took over the states. (In Brazil, state governments had far more power and influence than those in the United States.)

A number of uprisings by those who opposed the dictatorship were ruthlessly put down. The crackdowns became known as the "dirty war," and its atrocities would haunt Brazil for decades as families and friends of the victims futilely sought justice.

Despite all this horror, the military regimes were able to improve the economy. The Brazilian "miracle" had begun.

7

Life Under the Military

The Brazilian "miracle," like many things Brazilian, was doomed to failure. However, it was a fun ride while it lasted. The economy grew at an annual rate of nearly 11 percent. By 1973, Brazil was exporting $10 billion worth of products, compared with $3 billion in 1968. At least for the upper and middle classes, life was good. The poor people, as always, didn't get much of a taste of the new prosperity.

The generals who now ran the country launched 33 huge projects, each costing $1 billion or more, in the fields of industry, communications, agriculture, mining, transportation, energy, steel, and petrochemicals. The projects also included a series of hydro-electric dams in the Amazon Basin that flooded millions of acres of forest and jungle, creating what environmentalists called an ecological disaster.

This 1985 photo shows the charred remains of a Brazilian rain forest, after burning. Throughout the decades, deforestation, precipitated by the attempts of the country's many poor to make a living at agriculture, as well as the many greedy to make more than their share, has proceeded without regulation.

Brazilians, though, like big projects. The bigger they are, the better the Brazilians feel about their country and themselves. It is as if the projects let the people believe, if only for a little while, that their country might be as great as they have always thought it ought to be. This has been called the "pharaonic complex," a reference to the ancient pharaohs, or rulers, of Egypt, famous for building immense structures, like the Sphinx and the pyramids.

Of course, the Brazilian projects required the borrowing of immense sums of money, and while borrowing large sums of money may make life pleasant for the moment, the debt has to be paid some day.

It was during the years of the "miracle" that the development of the Amazon Basin began. The basin, in the northern part of Brazil, is the location of the rain forest, the destruction of which has cost many lives and brought on international protests.

The Amazon Basin covers an area of more than 1.3 million square miles (3.4 million sq km), or 42 percent of the entire country. It consists of forest and jungle and is rich in natural resources.

President Castelo Branco called for "Operation Amazonia." People were given tax breaks and easy credit to move to the region. The population there grew from 2.5 million in 1960 to 8.5 million by 1985. Cities and towns grew and thrived.

ENVIRONMENTAL DAMAGE

To develop the region with industry, farms, and ranches, vast acres of forest were burned and cleared. The hydroelectric dam projects were to provide power for the development.

The damage to the world's environment is too vast to be measured accurately. Nobody knows for sure what the development has done to the air, the ozone layer, and the people who live there. But one thing is certain: It cannot be good.

The first step in the development of the Amazon Basin was the building of roads. Army engineers built a transcontinental highway and a network of other roads. The highways opened vast stretches of the region to development in agriculture, cattle raising, mining, and other activities.

The way of life of the Indians who lived in those areas was severely damaged. The native people were afflicted with diseases they had never known before, and those made homeless could be seen begging along the roads. Sometimes they fought back, and were slaughtered.

The murder of Chico Mendes in 1988 created a new martyr to the cause of saving the rain forest. He was a rubber-tapper, a worker who taps latex from the rubber trees. He launched a campaign to save the Amazon, and encouraged many others to follow him. A rancher ordered him killed, and Mendes instantly became a hero.

Activists from all over the world came to Brazil to carry on his work. Money poured in from many sources. The killers lived to regret creating a hero whom environmentalists could rally around and gain strength from.

OPEC STRIKES

The ruling generals encouraged American and European industrialists to come to Brazil where they would not have to worry about expensive anti-pollution systems. When environmentalists complained, the generals had an easy answer: The "pollution of poverty" could only be solved by economic development.

The regime used methods to encourage development similar to those used to draw people to the Amazon Basin: tax breaks and easy credit.

It all went sour in 1973 when the Organization of Petroleum Exporting Countries (OPEC), made up of many Arab countries, jacked up the price of oil because of the support by Western nations (including the United States) for Israel during the Yom Kippur War. That year Egypt and Syria attacked Israel on the Jewish holiday.

The price increase (another jolt occurred in 1980) caused oil and gasoline shortages throughout the world. There were long lines at gas stations in the United States and elsewhere brought on by the increase. Brazil was especially hard hit because it was the third world's leading oil importer. Its rate of growth dropped, inflation soared, and the balance-of-payments (the difference between a country's export and import revenues) ballooned. The debt to foreign countries passed the $100 billion mark.

Soon, Brazil was in a deep recession. The "miracle" was over.

THE MILITARY'S BAD IMAGE

The generals did not know what to do. They decided it was time to return to civilian rule. They were further pushed in that direction by a growing feeling among the people that the military was not their friend. The generals had managed to convince people early on that they had stamped out the Communist menace and restored law and order. But the "dirty war" gave them a bad image.

The death in 1973 of a student activist named Alexandre Vannucchi Leme, who died after being arrested for subversive activities and tortured, led to massive demonstrations. More than 3,000 people attended his funeral. In 1975, a journalist named Vladimir Herzog was tortured to death, and the public was outraged. The image of the military was severely damaged. Officers hesitated to wear their uniforms in public.

The last of the generals who ran the country was João Batista de Oliveira Figueiredo. He was most concerned with making sure that no one was punished for the "dirty war" outrages, including both the victims and the torturers and killers.

In 1979, he issued a general amnesty for all participants; political prisoners were released, and people driven into exile were allowed to return. It was estimated that the law benefited 4,650 people.

He also did away with the contrived two-party system that the military regime had set up to give the appearance of representative government. The new law had its drawbacks, however. It eventually led to the formation of so many parties that confusion and chaos sometimes reigned, and governments were stymied in trying to get work done. The American system, in which two major parties compete with each other for control, is considered far more efficient.

Figueiredo was, in many ways, a sad figure. Some consider him the worst president Brazil ever had. During his regime from 1979 to 1985, the country suffered a severe recession. Brazil set a world record for foreign debt, and in 1984, it had a 223.8 percent inflation rate, a record at the time. When he left office, he said, "I want people to forget me."

His disapproval rating was 70 percent. After his death in his Rio apartment on Christmas Eve 1999, at the age of 81, no government official of any prominence attended his funeral. President Cardoso, although he was in Rio at the time, sent his Army chief to the funeral.

THE SMELL OF A HORSE

Figueiredo had been an athletic man, but two years after he became president, he suffered a heart attack. From then on, his health went steadily downhill. He went to Cleveland, Ohio, for bypass surgery.

In 1995, he lost 60 percent of his vision to a procedure in a Rio hospital, but he didn't sue. He seemed resigned to his fate, and to be forgotten. "Even the fair-weather friends have disappeared," he lamented.

He left the presidency almost by the back door. He refused to pass the presidential sash to his successor, José Sarney, whom he despised. He had even called Sarney a traitor.

Figueiredo died alone, forgotten, and filled with resentment. Even his wife had stopped speaking to him. She made a habit of sleeping when he was awake to avoid having to talk with

Brazilian soldiers, family, and friends accompany the coffin of General João Baptista Figueiredo, Brazil's last military dictator, to his grave in Rio de Janeiro, December 1999. During his 1978–1985 presidency, Figueiredo sped up the transition to democracy begun by his predecessor.

him. She tore up his Christmas cards, and refused to allow visitors to see him.

Figueiredo loved horses more than people. He once said, "The smell of a horse, the sweet smell of a horse, is better than the smell of people."

He requested that his coffin be escorted to the cemetery by cavalrymen, and he once said that he didn't want to go to heaven, "because they only have one horse there and that's a mere nag, the one ridden by St. George."

In the presidential election of 1985, the military did not put forth a candidate. The civilian opposition put up Tancredo Neves, governor of the state of Minas Gerais, who had served as prime minister when Brazil tried the parliamentary form of government. Neves won over the military leaders by assuring them he would treat them with respect and forgive and forget past evils.

But once again, things went awry. Neves collapsed on the eve of his inauguration and was rushed to a military hospital. He died on April 21, 1985, having never assumed office. The country was shocked. Neves had been seen as the best man to bring the country back from its 21 dark years of military rule.

The reaction to the fatal illness of the 75-year-old Neves was an example of a Brazilian tendency to believe in miracles. As he underwent a series of abdominal surgeries, Roman Catholics, Protestants, and followers of various African-born religions prayed for divine intervention. Not only did they *ask* for a miracle, many of them *expected* it. As reported in a *New York Times* article, "A man dragged a large wooden cross along the hospital sidewalk. Another followed, flagellating himself with a whip. People have walked by on wounded knees, fumbling rosaries, praying, chanting out loud."

As described by Joseph A. Page in his book *The Brazilians*, many people believed a widely circulated report that the cause of Neves's death was an infection he contracted from one of many onlookers who were allowed in the operating room during his surgeries.

A BAD OMEN

Neves's death was a particular blow to Brazilians because of the euphoria that had attended the end of the brutal military dictatorship. They yearned for someone skilled enough to lead them into a new era. They had believed that Neves was the man.

Joseph Page described one example of this yearning in the birth of the first child on New Year's Day 1985. The boy was named

Tancredinho in Neves's honor. But three months later, the baby, who lived in a Rio de Janeiro slum, died of pneumonia and dehydration. To superstitious Brazilians, it was a bad omen.

Vice President José Sarney became president. He was the first civilian president since the military took over the country in 1964, but nobody had wanted him for the post. He had backed the military regime, and had practically no support. However, he did not do too badly, considering the condition of Brazil when he took over.

Sarney launched the Cruzado Plan, an anti-inflationary scheme that included wage and price freezes. The inflation rate fell to 2 percent a month, consumer confidence rose, tax revenues increased, and the economy recovered.

But the plan ended disastrously in 1987 when the government had to lift the cap on prices because of serious shortages of food and other consumer goods.

The economy overheated, prices soared, and inflation reached 1,038 percent. At that rate, the joke went, a person would go to the store with his money in a shopping basket, and come home with his purchases in his wallet.

(One of the ways Brazilian governments over the years dealt with a shortage of funds was simply to print more money. This always devastated the economy, and the money became worthless.)

PRESIDENTIAL SPENDING

Sarney had run out of ideas. The press reported ever-increasing corruption scandals that reached from the lowest government levels all the way up to the administration. There was public outrage when Sarney flew 150 guests to Paris at government expense to celebrate the bicentennial of the French Revolution. People were starving and the administration was off celebrating an event that had nothing to do with Brazil.

Crime was also out of control. Gangs of drug dealers had taken over entire areas of slums. They became the government, even providing some municipal services. The rich hid behind barbed-wire fences. The poor, always the major victims of crime, had no place to hide.

Sarney was not able to stop another kind of disaster—the construction of immense dams in the Amazon Basin, which flooded millions of acres of forest and jungle. The projects were started under the military dictatorship.

One of these dams, at Balbina, on a tributary of the Amazon River, 90 miles (145 km) north of Manaus, turned out to be a highly questionable project. It flooded 900 square miles (2,330 sq km) of jungle, but provided only a miniscule amount of power, hardly meriting its $750 million cost. The criticism of the project made President Sarney decide to boycott the dam's inauguration ceremony.

A new Constitution—the country's eighth—was enacted on October 5, 1988, after a two-year struggle. The minutely detailed document provided for many new freedoms, including giving labor organizations the right to strike and bargain for labor contracts. Censorship was abolished. The president was forbidden to enact laws by decree (without going through Congress). The voting age was lowered to 16.

The Constitution also capped annual interest rates at 12 percent, which was seen as something of a joke. Such a cap could not possibly happen in a country where the monthly interest rate was at least twice that amount.

ANTI-SMOKING CAMPAIGN
One provision of the new document concerned presidential elections. If no candidate received an absolute majority of the vote, a run-off would be held between the two leading vote-getters.

But the Constitution ignored the serious problem of unfair representation in the Congress. One-third of the population controlled two-thirds of the members of the Chamber of Deputies, giving politicians from the rural areas more power than those of the coastal cities.

An example cited by Page was that a deputy from São Paulo, one of the world's most populous cities, would need more than 200,000 votes to be elected, while one from Roraima, a state in Amazonia, would need only about 5,000.

Despite his shortcomings, Sarney managed to make lasting contributions to the health of Brazil's citizens. He pushed through a law guaranteeing that AIDS sufferers could get the drugs and treatments they needed. And he launched an anti-smoking campaign.

The presidential election of 1989 was approaching. It would be the first time Brazilians could cast votes for a president in almost 30 years. Among the favored candidates was Luiz Inácio Lula da Silva. He was the man seen as the only candidate who could really claim to represent the working people and the poor. It looked as if he might have a chance.

This terrified a lot of people, especially the elite, because Lula, as every Brazilian called him, represented the left wing, just a shade this side of Communism, in a lot of people's minds.

Would the elite finally have to share power with the workers and the poor?

Was the country as a whole ready for radical change?

The answer in 1989 was no. But the fact that Lula got 32 million votes in that election—47 percent of the ballots cast —even while losing, was evidence that something different was about to happen to Brazil.

8

Lula in Charge

Brazilians have always looked for a "Messiah figure," someone who would guide the country to the greatness they think it has the potential for. But every leader the people thought might be that person has proven to be a disappointment—from the emperors of the eighteenth and nineteenth centuries, to the duly elected presidents and the military dictators who forced themselves on the public.

Nobody had been able to sustain the Brazilian "miracle." Was one of the problems the fact that the previous leaders had been either members of the elite, if not royalty, or generals?

Now, with the election of Luiz Inácio Lula da Silva in 2002, it was the workers' opportunity. Like all who went before him, Lula had his work cut out for him. Nothing in Brazil, it seems, is ever easy.

In his election campaigns, he stressed his dedication to *mudança,* the Portuguese word for change. He claimed that when elected, he would begin rebuilding Brazil "starting from scratch."

That sounded to many like an impractical idea. Each new president was faced with the cards that were dealt him by the previous administration—not always a happy prospect, but a realistic one.

Lula said he would need more than his four-year term to get the job done, but his reelection prospects in 2006 will depend on how the electorate views his accomplishments. Only his immediate predecessor, Fernando Cardoso, was able to persuade the voters to give him a second term. Even though Cardoso left many voters disappointed, he started a number of programs that some experts believed were worth continuing.

In a survey in February 2003, a little more than a month after Lula was inaugurated, *The Economist,* the respected British financial weekly, argued as much. "Brazil's frequent political ruptures since independence from Portugal in 1822 led to a lack of follow-through in pursuing public policies that has cost the country dear, ..." the paper wrote. It went on to say that Cardoso "made a good start on overcoming such debilitating short-termism."

EDUCATION IMPROVED

The problem had always been that each new president brought his own agenda to office, and had frequently been left a mess by his predecessor. Instead of taking what good the man before him had accomplished, the new leaders also wanted to "start from scratch."

But *The Economist* noted that Cardoso had achieved a great deal in a number of areas, most notably education. During his regime, the paper pointed out, "Brazil achieved near-universal primary schooling for the first time in its history, and a surge in enrollments to secondary and university education."

He engineered a "fiscal-responsibility" law, which put an end to the spending excesses of state and local governments. On the other hand, he could not seem to get the justice minister he wanted. He ran through nine of them.

"Murder, armed robbery, and other violent crimes continued at shockingly high rates," *The Economist* wrote, "aided and abetted by a still inefficient and corruption-riddled police and judiciary."

Many of Lula's political opponents agreed early on to give the man a chance. They included Cardoso's center-right Social Democracy Party, and the biggest partner in Cardoso's ruling coalition, the Brazilian Democratic Movement Party. Leaders promised to back Lula on reforms vital to the national interest.

But those in Congress must abide by the wishes of the voters who put them in office, not to mention the political bosses, the lobbyists, and everyone else who seeks to influence them.

Lula described himself as a "great negotiator," able to sit down with friend and foe alike and gain compromise and cooperation. He created some councils of leaders from many segments of society to do just that. They had grand-sounding names—the Council of Economic and Social Development and the National Labor Forum. He would sit down with members of these groups and try to work out problems of mutual concern.

Among the problems he inherited from Cardoso's administration was the enormous government debt of $260 billion. That amounted to 56 percent of Brazil's gross domestic product (the total of the country's goods and services). A lot of those loans were short-term, which meant they constantly had to be renewed. Most of the debt was tied either to short-term interest rates, or to the real's value against the dollar. Both were strongly affected by investors' fears that Brazil might default.

The more fearful lenders are, the higher the costs of borrowing. It is a situation similar to the problems of a person with poor credit trying to borrow money. Somebody might lend him the money, but the lenders will charge much higher interest rates and impose other restrictions to make sure they get their money back.

A NEIGHBOR'S TROUBLES

When it appeared that the left-wing Lula was going to be the next president, investors became really worried. There was this great, looming debt, and along comes a man with radical ideas. There were predictions that bankers and other business leaders would flee the country.

More nerves were jangled by the example of next-door neighbor Argentina. The government there defaulted on a record $141 billion late in 2001. The economic collapse of Argentina, which had been building for about a decade, led to chaos in that country of 39 million.

There was rioting in the streets when bank accounts were frozen and people could not get to their savings. Twenty-two people were killed in a December 2001 riot. Federal and local governments in Argentina paid their workers with something like Monopoly, or play, money, which few businesses would accept. The government was bankrupt. President Fernando de la Rua was forced to resign. Although Argentina's economy began to recover, shortages of electricity and gas early in 2004 brought on more emergencies.

Visions of what happened in Argentina made Brazil's creditors wonder, "Could it happen here?"

Worries were eased when the International Monetary Fund (IMF) came through with a $30 billion loan. Of course, a country does not get IMF money for nothing. The agency insists on measures to stabilize the economy, sometimes spelling out in detail what must be done. That was why Lula initially opposed the IMF loan. He didn't like the idea of an outside agency butting into Brazil's business. But reality forced him to change his views.

The *real* and Brazilian bonds continued to recover. Lula also appointed some respected business and financial figures to key government jobs.

By international standards, Brazil is a middle-income country, rather than a poor country. But the unequal income distribution is enormous. The poorest 50 percent of the population account for 10 percent of the national income, and so do the richest 1 percent. Nineteen percent of Brazilian households lacked running water.

MINORITY GOVERNMENT

Although Lula's approval ratings declined after his first year in office, he remained popular enough, in most observers' eyes, to continue with his reforms. For instance, his "Zero Hunger" campaign called for a kind of food-stamp program for the poor. It was having mixed results, but it was seen as a start on his promise to end hunger.

As long as he remained popular, members of Congress would feel obligated to support his reforms. But they could easily turn on a leader they saw losing the support of the public.

Lula's Workers' Party did not have a majority in Congress, so he had to rely on other political parties to help him. If they decided to join his government, he would have a majority and the road ahead would be smoother. Cardoso, with his majority in Congress, was unable to push through reforms he wanted in the areas of pensions, taxes, labor laws, and justice, so some observers wondered, how could Lula do so, with a minority in Congress? Actually, Lula could not even rely on his own party because it still had unreformed radicals who did not share all of his vision for Brazil. Some felt that the once-radical Lula had deserted them.

On the other hand, Lula did not have to bow to the conservative elite, as Cardoso and many other elected presidents had had to do. The rich conservatives contributed nothing to Lula's election success, so he owed them nothing.

Of course, Brazilians believe in magic and miracles, and magic and miracles are instantaneous events. The people could easily run out of patience when facing the fact that

Lula's reforms, or anybody's reforms, take time and patience. Brazilians are not a patient people. But they are optimistic. They will give a new leader the benefit of the doubt.

The Economist in its survey described a "nightmare" scenario in which Brazil followed its Argentinian neighbor into disaster. The result would be rising poverty, crime, and unrest. Lula would go down in Brazilian history as another failure, one who could not deliver the promise of a great nation, one who turned out not to be the expected "Messiah," but just an ordinary mortal unable to overcome the staggering problems of this sprawling nation.

Lula was born on October 27, 1945, in Garanhuns, a city in the southern highlands of the state of Pernambuco, which used to be dependent on slave labor. Jokers said that the state motto should have been, "Visit Pernambuco before we all starve to death."

The president at that time was General Eurico Dutra, who served between the two terms of Getúlio Vargas. Dutra was a conservative who did not like to try anything new. He slowed down the process of industrialization and opened the country to a flood of imported goods. Prices rose and there was general unrest, until Vargas made a surprising comeback and was elected president again in 1950.

FATHER RETURNS

Lula (the name means "squid" in Portuguese) was the sixth of 23 children of Aristides Inácio da Silva, a poor farmer. Not all of those children had the same mother. Aristides was not a man to stay with one woman, or one family, for very long. In fact, shortly after Lula's birth, he left Lula's mother, Eurídice, for another woman, and headed south. Lula was one of seven children born to Eurídice.

His father moved to Santos, near São Paulo, where he got a job loading sacks of coffee onto cargo ships. In 1949, he returned to Garanhuns with the other woman and two children he had with her. He stayed for only 20 days, but during that time impregnated Eurídice again. He then returned south, taking two of Lula's older brothers with him.

There is no record of the emotional trauma Aristides's comings and goings must have caused the da Silva household, but it can be imagined.

Three years later, Eurídice received a letter supposedly written by Aristides urging her to come to him in Santos. It turned out the letter had been written by one of the older boys, who missed his mother. Eurídice packed her children into a *paus-de-arara*, which means "parrot perch," on an open flatbed truck. And they embarked on a grueling and dusty 2,000-mile (3,219-km) journey over some of the worst roads in the country.

A SURPRISE ARRIVAL

Aristides was surprised by the sudden arrival of the family he had deserted, but he recovered quickly. He helped them find a place to live, and then divided his time between his two families. Eurídice finally got fed up with the arrangement, and moved her family to São Paulo. Accommodations there were not very pleasant. The mother and her eight children, plus three cousins, lived in one room in the back of a bar. They had to share a bathroom with the bar's owners.

To help support his family, Lula took to the streets of that immense city. He shined shoes, sold peanuts and pastries, and otherwise scrounged for food money. He eventually got a steady job in a dry-cleaning factory.

He managed to attend school long enough to learn to read and write. He was the only one of his brothers and sisters to get even that much of an education. ("Lula" was a childhood nickname, but he had it legally incorporated into his full name in later years.)

At the age of 14, Lula went to work in a factory that produced screws. He attended a state-run technical school where he learned to be a mechanic. He worked the night shift at the factory, and was unable to get much sleep in that crowded one-room apartment. Lula was probably drowsy when he lost the little finger on his left hand while operating a machine press.

BRASÍLIA BUILT

This was a relatively good time for Brazil. President Juscelino Kubitschek had commissioned Oscar Niemeyer and Lúcio Costa to build Brazil's dream capital at Brasília.

There wasn't much of a democracy, votes were bought and sold as always, but there were certain civil liberties. People like Lula who could read and write–and they were quite rare among working folk of the time–had access to a relatively free press.

Kubitschek, the president with the motto, "Fifty years of progress in five," started an ambitious industrial development program. But wages remained low, and the people on the bottom rung of the economic ladder were still suffering. The gap between the haves and the have-nots widened, the old Brazilian story. In 1957, fully one-fourth of Rio's residents lived in *favelas* (squatter settlements).

When the military took over the government in 1964, a recession dimmed the economy. The slump caused Lula to lose his job. That was when he took the job as a metalworker in the factory in São Bernardo do Campo, just outside São Paulo, and began his union activities.

YOUTH TAKES OVER

Ironically, some of the military regime's policies were what gave labor unions the spark they needed to rise to power. The regime purged militant union leaders, opening the door to a new generation of young workers to take over. By outlawing strikes, the regime forced unions to concentrate on bread-and-butter issues—wages, benefits, and working conditions. The new leaders came in closer contact with the rank-and-file workers, in contrast to the older leaders who sometimes had no contact with the workers. Men were

Renowned Brazilian architect Oscar Niemeyer stands near the double arch of a building under construction in Brasília, the preplanned capital of Brazil, which he designed under President Kubitschek. Plans for the city were in the works as early as 1823, but Kubitschek forged ahead and built the city to ensure inland development and to restore national confidence to the Brazilian people.

moving from the shop floor into union leadership positions for the first time.

In addition, community groups were forming in the slums. This was a novelty for Brazil, where the poor traditionally had no voice in public affairs. These groups started out as religious organizations formed because of a lack of priests in Brazil. But they gradually became actual community groups in which poor people could get together and try to do something about their plight. They chose their own leaders from their organizations.

In combination with the new look of the labor unions, the poor and the workers were beginning to assert themselves even under the harsh rule of the military dictatorships.

They became the "voice of the voiceless."

9

Sports and Beauty

It might seem odd to Americans to realize how important soccer is to Brazil. Americans enjoy their baseball, football, basketball, ice-hockey—as well as soccer—but the passion generated by soccer in Brazil, which has led to violent death and suicides, is difficult to understand.

American football fans, for instance, might have a bad day after a loss by their favorite team, especially in a crucial game, but the fans are not going to brood about it for years, even decades, as Brazilians do. And nobody in America is going to kill himself because his team lost a game. But that has happened in Brazil.

After Brazil won the World Cup in 1970, 44 people died at a wild celebration organized by Emílio Médici, then the president and an avid soccer fan.

Soccer in Brazil, where it is called football, also has political ramifications, and it is seen as a reflection of the society as a whole. Clubs represent various social levels, from workers to the elite. The Corinthians team, of which President Luiz Inácio Lula da Silva was a longtime member and an honorary lifetime director, was a strong supporter of the government. The team was founded in São Paulo by workers, and was the only soccer club still dominated by the working class.

Lula not only supported soccer and followed it religiously, he played it. Even in his late 50s, he and members of his government played regular matches on the presidential palace grounds. The practice was reminiscent of the touch football games in which members of John F. Kennedy's family famously engaged.

And Lula's soccer matches weren't just for fun. Like all soccer players, Lula and his associates played hard, and to win. In April 2003, Antonio Palocci, Brazil's finance minister, showed up in Congress on crutches. He had sustained the injury in one of Lula's "friendly" soccer matches.

PLUNDERING THE GAME

Unfortunately, soccer in Brazil had traditionally been run by a largely corrupt group of bosses called *cartolas,* meaning "top hats." They plundered the game and made themselves wealthy.

One of Lula's first acts after he became president in 2003 concerned soccer. His predecessor, Fernando Henrique Cardoso, had introduced temporary legislation to open up the soccer management to public scrutiny. Lula made it permanent. It is called the Law of Moralization in Sport.

On the same day in May 2003, Lula signed a "fans' bill of rights." The law contained some obvious provisions involving safety, hygiene, and ticketing. It also required the Brazilian Confederation of Football to hold at least one national competition in which the "teams know before it begins how many games they will play and who their opponents will be." It might

President Lula da Silva holds a personalized Corinthians soccer team jersey during a meet in Brasília, Brazil, February 2003. Brazil's working class supports the Corinthians and da Silva, both underdogs. Lula da Silva's supporters were rewarded during Brazil's 2002 presidential election, when they put da Silva in office. The Brazilian president was a longtime member of the Corinthians and is the club's honorary lifetime director. The Corinthians team was founded by São Paulo workers and is the only soccer club still dominated by the working class.

seem ridiculous for this to be a law, rather than simple common sense or part of the confederation's regulations, but in Brazil it was needed. The cartolas had politicized soccer to the extent that they would include teams in the league as political favors, and no one knew who was playing which team and where. At one point, ninety-four teams were in the league.

The law did away with the playoffs for the national championship, in which the winner was not always the best team. Now, all teams play each other, and the winner is the team with the best combined results, just like the major European leagues.

The great Brazilian star, Pelé, was Cardoso's minister of sport, and he tried and failed to reform the game. The fans' law provoked the league leadership to threaten a shutdown, but Lula stood firm and, after a forty-eight-hour standoff, the league bosses changed their minds.

Lula is the first passionate soccer fan since Médici. Fernando Collor, who beat Lula in his first bid for the presidency in 1989, was not considered a true fan. He was a cartola, and president of his local football team, often a springboard into politics.

The Corinthians had always been more than a football team. It was at a Corinthians match, in front of 100,000 people, that a banner urging amnesty for political prisoners during the military dictatorship was displayed for the first time. A Corinthian fan group called Hawks of the Faithful was the first to organize itself politically so as to make demands on the club's management. A soccer player named Socrates organized a movement called Corinthians Democracy, which fought for the rights of players. Socrates was a member of the Workers' Party, and later joined Lula in calling for reforms in government.

SOCCER ARRIVES

Soccer was introduced in Brazil in 1894 by Charles "Nipper" Miller. Miller, the son of a Scottish banker, was born in São Paulo in 1875. He went to school in England and learned the game. When he came back home in 1894, he had two

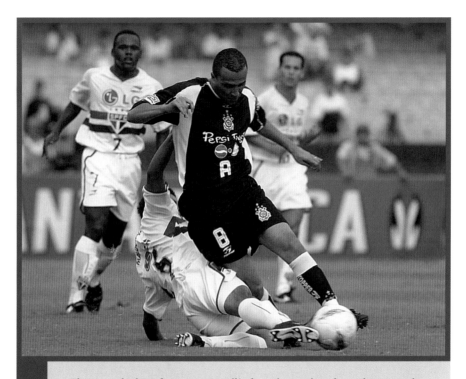

The popularity of soccer, Brazil's favorite national pastime, can be compared to football and fans in the United States. Brazilian fans are so dedicated to their sport that some were reported to have committed suicide when their country lost the World Cup in 1950. Here professional soccer teams Corinthians and São Paulo battle it out during a match for the Rio–São Paulo first division tournament at the Morumbi stadium in São Paulo, Brazil, May 2002. Over the years, Brazil has won several World Cups.

soccer balls with him. He was rather appalled to find out that Brazilians had cricket clubs, but nobody played soccer.

He taught the game to whomever would listen to him. He formed the São Paulo Athletic Club, the first soccer club in Brazil. Its game with Mackenzie College on June 19, 1899, was Brazil's first soccer match. Miller's club won, 1–0.

And the rest, as they say, is history. Miller died in 1953, five years before Brazil won its first World Cup championship.

Old-timers in Brazil still talk about the disastrous World Cup game played on July 16, 1950, before 200,000 overconfident fans in Maracana Stadium in Rio. Brazil was highly favored to beat Uruguay, and the game seemed a mere formality before Brazil would be crowned king of the soccer world.

Brazil scored first, but early in the second half, Uruguay scored and the game was tied at 1–1. This seemed to unnerve the Brazilian players, who apparently had not expected Uruguay to fight back. They went quickly from cocky overconfidence to wary caution.

As Joseph A. Page describes the final minutes of the game in his book, *The Brazilians*, a Uruguayan winger named Alcides Ghiggia, nicknamed Perrito (Puppy), "worked a perfect give-and-go pass with a teammate and darted past his defender, Bigode.

"Deep on the right side, he pushed the ball into the penalty area. Juvenal, another Brazilian defender, retreated in a desperate but tardy effort to mark his opponent but left a Uruguayan attacker free in front of the net.

"The Brazilian goalkeeper, Barbosa, anticipated a centering pass, but Ghiggia opted to shoot from a very difficult angle, and he put the ball past the goalie on the short side and into the twine."

THE LIVING DEAD

The 200,000 people in the stands, and a radio audience that probably included the rest of the nation, were stunned. A reporter said the fans exited the stadium in slow motion, "a battalion of the living dead." Another writer said the Brazilian team left the field "like sleepwalkers."

The extent of the catastrophe is difficult for non-Brazilians to understand. National honor had been at stake, and was crushed upon the soccer field. There were reports that some fans killed themselves. Others vowed never to set foot in Maracana Stadium again.

The players entered a nightmare that would last for decades. The government secret police called Barbosa to its headquarters and asked him if he was a Communist. Juvenal couldn't bring himself to leave his house for weeks. Fingers of blame were pointed everywhere. The players blamed each other and their coach. Barbosa contended that Ghiggia meant to pass the ball, but it somehow found its way into the goal—accidentally. He had to come up with some excuse to try to erase the phrase, "Barbosa's chicken," that threatened to haunt him the rest of his days. (*Chicken* is Brazilian soccer slang for an easy shot that somehow eludes the goalkeeper.)

Soccer stars were revered in Brazil as near god-like figures. One of the first was Arthur Friedenreich, son of a German father and a mixed-race mother. Called the "Tiger," he scored 1,329 goals in his career, a record not even Pelé could match.

Another was Leonidas da Silva, called the "Black Diamond," who invented the "bicycle kick," in which he performed a half somersault backward and at the same time kicked the ball in the opposite direction from which he was facing. He put on a spectacular show during the World Cup tournament in France in 1938, although Brazil lost in the semifinals to the eventual winner, Italy.

A STAR IS BORN

When Brazil lost the heartbreaker to Uruguay in 1950, Pelé, whose real name was Edson Arantes do Nascimento, was a skinny 9-year-old boy living in Bauru in the state of São Paulo. At 15, he became a star for the Santos team and soon attracted national attention. He and Mane Garrincha, a 24-year-old with a deceptive dribbling style, were the stars when Brazil won the World Cup in Sweden in 1958. The victory helped ease Brazilians' pain over the 1950 disaster.

Brazil won World Cup championships in 1962 in Chile, and in 1970 in Mexico. Brazil became the first country ever to win three world titles. President Médici seemed to take personal credit for the 1970 victory. A few days before the team's departure for the tournament, he had the coach, João Saldanha, fired for resisting the president's demand that his favorite striker be part of the team.

The Brazilian style of soccer delighted experts of the game. One described it as "soccer with a smile, fluid, entertaining, immensely skilled and acrobatic."

Brazilians had to wait until 1994 for their next World Cup victory in Pasadena, California.

Pelé went on to a successful business career and played soccer for several years for the New York Cosmos. Garrincha made a mess of his post-soccer life, and drank himself to death in 1983. The soccer stadium in Brasília is named for him, as are other fields where the game is played.

For many years, soccer was the *only* sport in Brazil. Every boy, they said, went to sleep with a soccer ball under his bed. Now, the ball might just as likely be a basketball. One of Brazil's favorite sports heroes was a basketball player named Oscar Schmidt. He was a long-range gunner and scoring phenomenon who led Brazil to its historic victory over the United States (where basketball was invented) in the 1987 Pan American Games.

When Schmidt retired in 2003 at the age of 45, he had amassed an amazing record in his 26-year career. He had scored a total of 49,703 points with various clubs and Brazil's national club. He played in five Olympics, and was the top scorer in three, sinking a total of 1,093 points in Olympics play. In the win over a favored United States team at the Pan Am Games, he scored forty-six points to lead his team. Most of his shots were made from three-point range.

Three Brazilians have played for National Basketball Association teams in the United States: Alex Garcia, for the San Antonio Spurs; Leandro Mateus Barbosa, for the Phoenix Suns; and Maybyner "Nene" Hilario, for the Denver Nuggets. The NBA has been promoting itself in Brazil for a number of years, and millions of Brazilians watch games on satellite television. Youngsters started to wear NBA team jerseys and caps in the streets, and to play the game on the growing number of courts at schools and playgrounds in cities big and small.

BEAUTIFUL PEOPLE

The Brazilian passion for health and beauty is well known. The young men and women who exhibit themselves on the sparkling beaches along the Atlantic Ocean, and parade nearly naked at Carnival time, must be in good shape. Especially since volleyball is a favorite sport along the beaches.

One of the most famous beaches in the world is Copacabana in Rio de Janeiro. It is hard to think of Rio without picturing the beautiful setting of the beach with Sugar Loaf Mountain in the background.

Oddly, Copacabana wasn't always what it is today, and, even odder, Brazilians had no interest in exposing their skin to the sun and water until about the 1920s. In fact, it was hard to get to Copacabana Beach from the city until the opening of the Real Grandeza Tunnel in 1892, and the introduction of regular tram service. The wealthy had no interest in sunbathing there or anywhere else. Poor people might take an occasional cleansing dip, or go to the shore to make an offering to Jemanja, the goddess of the sea. But that was about it. The elite wanted to preserve their white skins, because it set them apart from the poor workers who had to struggle under the blazing sun to make a living.

Occasionally, a doctor would prescribe a quick dip in the sea, but only around dawn before the sun became too strong. To sit in the sun was considered a serious breach of social etiquette. But in 1886, the famous French actress Sarah Bernhardt arrived in Rio to star in "Frou-Frou" and "The Lady of the Camellias" at the San Pedro Theatre. She shocked everyone by going to the beach in what was then considered a daring bathing suit—and *actually entering the water!* While she was in Rio, she spent

Brazilian hot spot Copacabana, one of the most famous beaches in the world. While much of Brazil languishes in poverty, the world's beautiful people enjoy this beach resort, made famous in 1923 by the construction of the Copacabana Palace Hotel by renowned French hotelier Octavo Guine. The hotel became a favorite stop for the well-to-do of Europe and the United States, and tourists eventually convinced the locals of the pleasures of sunbathing and swimming.

hours on the beach, enjoying the sun, the breeze and the wonderful view. Unheard of!

However, as more people began to follow Sarah's example, the city of Rio felt obliged to enact strict regulations for bathing in the sea. It was permitted only from 5 to 8 in the morning and 5 to 7 in the evening. An extra hour was allowed on Sundays and holidays. Beachgoers had to dress properly and behave themselves. A stiff fine or even jail time awaited people who made too much noise or bathed during the forbidden hours.

Foreign visitors were among the first to show that sunbathing and frolicking in the waves were fun, and Brazilians began to follow their example. The opening of the Copacabana Palace Hotel in 1923 turned the beach into a destination for tourists and locals and started it on its way to what it is now—a perennial beauty contest with skimpier and skimpier bathing attire.

BEAUTY BY SURGERY

As Brazilians age and confront the horrors of losing their looks, those who can afford it, turn to plastic surgery. Rio itself has become a mecca for cosmetic surgery. A recent survey showed that as many as 2,000 such surgeries were performed every month. The total annual cost was about $120 million.

Warren Hoge, a *New York Times* reporter, once wrote, "Looks count for almost everything in Rio society because very little else is in contention. . . . One can spend long sunny days on the beaches and at the clubs where the rich idle and never see anyone reading."

One of the most prominent of the hundreds of plastic surgeons who abound in Brazil is Ivo Pitanguy. He rose to the status of a celebrity through his ability to restore beauty to his patients with his skillful scalpel. Pitanguy was featured in a *New York Times* profile called "Dr. Vanity," and an American cable network produced a TV documentary about him entitled, "The Man With the Golden Touch."

WORSE THAN DEATH

He found his life's work after a devastating circus fire in the city of Niteroi, across the Guanabara Bay from Rio on December 17, 1961. Some 2,500 spectators, mostly poor people, were trapped beneath a burning tent. Many victims were children. The dead numbered 323, but many of the survivors were horribly disfigured by the fire.

Pitanguy, already a plastic surgeon working in a Rio hospital, rushed to the scene to help the injured. He worked day and night without rest. This experience determined his destiny. He came to realize that physical appearance can be as important as life itself. Some of his patients expressed a wish to die when they saw what the flames had done to them.

People have come from all over the world to be treated by Pitanguy. He has never revealed his patients' identities, but some very prominent actresses and other celebrities in America and abroad have expressed their gratitude to him for treating disfiguring injuries and keeping them looking young.

He is a well-rounded man. He speaks six languages fluently, holds a black belt in karate, and hobnobs with the socially prominent. He owned his own island, where he maintained a nature sanctuary and once entertained President Jimmy Carter.

Pitanguy, who likes to be called "Professor," believes there is beauty in everyone. All it needs to come out is a little help from his scalpel.

10

The First Year and Beyond

S imon Silva Vargas, a 70-year-old day laborer, looked down at the rich earth of a banana plantation that he and 200 other rural workers had just forced their way into, and said, "Brazil's land is in my veins, but none of it is mine."

It was a common sentiment among the hundreds of landless people who were taking over farms and plantations in 2004 as part of a movement to force the government of Luiz Inácio Lula da Silva to hurry up with promised land redistribution.

The group that Vargas was with showed up at dawn on March 20 outside the plantation near the oceanside village of Mangaratiba with machetes and hoes in hand. They cut the gate, stormed up the driveway, and began clearing the underbrush to make way for makeshift bamboo cabins.

World leaders at 2003 G8 Summit in Evian, France. Lula da Silva, one of a group of leaders from developing countries invited to the meeting's opening session on global issues, challenged the Group of Eight world powers to help create a fund to fight global hunger. "Hunger cannot wait," he said.

The raid was one of more than 100 land "occupations" organized by Brazil's Landless Workers' Movement in 2004. It was a continuation of a land-grab process that had been going on for years. The goal was to change the long-standing situation in Brazil in which less than 3 percent of the people control more than half of the fertile land. The land grabs were enjoying large public support because they were being done on a strictly nonviolent basis, and because only the rich were being inconvenienced.

The movement, known by the initials of its Portuguese name, MST, had been working for the poor for 20 years, but the land grabs were its biggest enterprise. The squatters usually occupied unused ground on large farms or plantations and stayed until they were officially expelled or succeeded in getting a land grant, although tactics began to change to include land that was in use.

After Lula was inaugurated in 2003, the movement slowed its occupations to wait to see if the new government would fulfill its promises to help the landless.

LAGGING BEHIND

But it looked as though Lula's administration was lagging behind the pace of land grants made by his predecessor, Fernando Cardoso. In 2003, government figures showed, only 37,000 families received grants, compared with an average of 66,000 a year during the previous eight years.

The government insisted the lag was necessary to ensure that the program was done correctly. But workers felt betrayed. After all, the MST was a strong supporter of Lula's candidacy in the 2002 election.

Also in April 2004, some 2,000 protesting farmers marched for days to get to Recife, the capital of Lula's home state of Pernambuco. "We want to show the whole world we need land so we can work," said Manuel José de Lima, 36, as he marched with the protesters. "The rich have most of the land in Brazil, and we just need some of it."

Other demonstrations that month occurred in Brasília; in Para, the state that takes up the eastern Amazon Basin; and in Rio de Janeiro.

"We'll deliver on the promise, but we also need to ensure that the land delivered will bear fruit," Guilherme Cassel, of the Ministry of Agricultural Development, told the *Boston Globe* in an interview in April 2004.

Landowners warned that the land grabs, if they increased, could damage the Brazilian economy's strongest sector, agriculture. That sector was booming in 2004. Part of the reason was that farmhands, truckers, and laborers came cheap. The average pay was $1 an hour, compared with the $9.36-an-hour average for farm laborers in the United States. The cheap labor costs enabled Brazilian farmers to raise cattle and grow crops for far less than an American farmer could. In Brazil, 30 percent of the population works in agriculture.

Land redistribution was only one of the many problems Lula's government faced as it began its second year in power.

DRUG HEROES

Last Easter, as tourists sipped drinks in Rio's exclusive Leblon district, machine-gun fire could plainly be heard from the scenic hills above. A turf war was raging between rival gangs seeking to dominate the Rocinha favela's drug market. At least a dozen people were killed.

Crime, fed by illicit drugs, was a problem that did not seem to have an easy solution. In some of the favelas, drug lords effectively ruled like a government bureaucracy. They had even been known to provide municipal services.

The problem was not confined to the drug cartels, but reached into many areas of Brazilian life where unemployment, lack of education, income inequality, and other problems led desperate people to commit crimes.

THE GOOD LIFE

The arrival of television in the country had placed before the eyes of millions of impoverished people images of the good life that they could not hope to achieve in any honest way. A slum child could earn five or 10 times the minimum wage running drugs, and there were no minimum-wage jobs anyway.

The government was trying. In 2004, it planned to provide low-income housing and grant property titles to 217,000 impoverished families. Lula's much-heralded "Zero Hunger" campaign, which granted subsidies to families if they sent children to school and for periodic health check-ups, was to move from the countryside, where it was being tested, to the cities, mainly in the favelas. Tough weapons legislation was passed in 2003, and both the federal police and the Air Force were stepping up air traffic controls to prevent drug-running from Colombia.

All of these programs were hampered by insufficient funds, as well as corruption on every level of the police and the judiciary.

As an example of the desperation of the authorities to stem the tide of drugs in the cities, there was a proposal to build walls around several of the favelas in Rio. As the *Financial Times* of London reported in April 2004, "The poverty- and crime-ridden favelas are already an embarrassing blemish on one of the worlds' most beautiful cities. Surrounding them with walls to turn them into living cemeteries would be a monument to segregation and inequality."

How drugs had taken hold of the people of the slums was evident in the way they reacted in 2004 when the police killed Luciano Barbosa da Silva, a drug lord known as Lulu. Hundreds of Rocinha residents mourned Lulu's death in April. After all, it was he, not the state, who took care of them. He helped them pay for basic needs.

CORRUPTION SCANDAL

Corruption in government has always been a problem in Brazil. But in 2004, Lula's administration was hit hard by a scandal involving the man who worked with Congress for the administration.

Waldomiro Diniz was videotaped two years before apparently soliciting hundreds of thousands of dollars in campaign contributions from the boss of an illegal numbers game in return for political favors. An investigation turned to Lula's most trusted aide, José Dirceu de Oliveira e Silva. Several party loyalists said that they had warned Dirceu and other party leaders of fund-raising irregularities but that they were either ignored or punished.

Dirceu told reporters, "This government doesn't steal or allow stealing."

Fernando Ferro, a Workers' Party member of Congress from Lula's home state of Pernambuco, said of Diniz, "I don't think he is the only one. Unfortunately, there is a lot of that in the Workers' Party, and there are a lot of people who are still going to create problems for the government."

If the scandal widened any further, Lula's administration would have been seriously distracted from its main missions.

URGING PATIENCE

As Lula completed his first year in January 2004, he was both praised and criticized for the pace of the reforms he had promised. He told factory workers in São Paulo, "I had to wait nine months to be born, eleven months to walk, and twelve months to talk. So why am I going to do things in a hurry?"

It is that kind of folksy approach to problems that kept Lula's popularity high even in the face of Brazil's continuing economic and other problems.

Marcos Coimbra, director of Vox Populi, a leading public opinion polling firm in Rio de Janeiro, said of Lula: "People don't just admire his biography or respect his political

President Lula da Silva speaks out against the U.S. war in Iraq during a speech in Brasília in March 2003. "Brazil," he said, "deplores the initiation of military action against Iraq."

trajectory, they genuinely like and trust Lula in a way that has no precedent for a Brazilian president.

"In spite of everything, he ends the year with more credibility and political capital than he started with because he has shown that someone with his origins is capable of running the government."

His approval rating at that time was 70 percent. In subsequent months, it declined, but the majority of Brazilians seemed willing to give him a fair chance.

PRAISE FOR LULA

On the international scene, James Wolfensohn, president of the World Bank, praised Lula's work in April 2004 as "the most important attempt perhaps in the world today to bring social equity to a very large country."

He said he believed Lula would succeed. Speaking to reporters at the spring meeting of the World Bank and International Monetary Fund in Washington, Wolfensohn said, "I often sound as if I'm on the payroll of President Lula. Let me start by saying I'm not."

As reported by Agence France-Presse, Wolfensohn praised Lula's efforts in "joining all segments of the country to a new objective, which is equity."

Talking to Brazilian reporters, Wolfensohn said Lula's bid for social equity was to put food on the table, and "to try and bring about what is a revolution in your country, which is that the rich and poor have to come together to get some more equitable distribution in order to have growth in the society."

He said quick results were not practical expectations. "I don't think he'll do that in one year and three months, or one year and five months," Wolfensohn said. "What we look for is consistency in what he's doing."

He said he believed Lula's financial and social-services teams "are actually making all the right steps."

"People want to see quick results, but they want to be responsible and I think they'll be effective," he said.

GROWTH PREDICTED

Another optimistic voice at the end of Lula's first year was that of Geraldo Carbone, president of BankBoston Brazil and chief operating officer of BankBoston Mexico. "I believe it is reasonable to expect growth in Brazil to total between 3 and 4 percent," he said, referring to 2004. "It is also reasonable to expect a continuing government commitment to keeping the inflation rate and external accounts under control.

"This, in fact, should provide the foundation for a more lasting economic growth cycle, which should bring with it a resumption of higher levels of investment by the end of 2004."

In the realm of foreign policy, Lula made some governments, including the United States, nervous by visiting his friend

Fidel Castro in Communist Cuba. On a trip to Libya, he described its dictator, Colonel Muammar el-Qaddafi, as a good friend. In Syria, he called for the United States to withdraw from Iraq.

But he had been lobbying for a permanent seat for Brazil on the United Nations Security Council in an effort to give Brazil more of a say in international relations.

HOPEFUL WAITING

As the soccer-playing president from humble origins continued with his second year in office, he faced many of the same problems that had baffled his predecessors—the unequal distribution of wealth and land, the country's vast diversity, its continuing heavy debt load, crime, poverty, unemployment, and volatile political parties.

Those problems weren't going to go away very soon. So far, most of his countrymen seemed willing to wait for him to keep his promises for reform.

But whether Lula succeeds or fails, observers saw his election as an important historical moment for Brazil. His Workers' Party was a breath of cool air in a nation where it was always assumed that the way to make Brazil better was to make the rich richer.

Because of Lula, for better or worse, it was unlikely that Brazil's future would be the same old tired story. Something different and new had happened, and the country would never be the same again.

1500   Brazil is discovered by Portuguese sailors.

1630   The Dutch invade Brazil. The Portuguese drive them out in 1654.

1750   Portugal and Spain sign a treaty recognizing Portugal's claim to Brazil.

1808   The Portuguese royal family rules Brazil and Portugal from Rio de Janeiro.

1822   Emperor Pedro I declares Brazil independent of Portugal.

1888   Slavery is abolished in Brazil.

1889   Brazil proclaims itself a republic.

1930   The military makes Getúlio Vargas president.

1934   A new Constitution gives women the right to vote.

1942   Brazil declares war on the Axis powers, and sends troops to fight in Europe.

1945   Brazil joins the United Nations.

1945   Luiz Inácio Lula da Silva is born in Garanhuns, Pernambuco.

1946   A new Constitution restores individual rights.

1950   Vargas returns for a second term.

1954   Vargas is forced out by the military, commits suicide.

1960   The capital moves from Rio de Janeiro to the new city of Brasília.

1964   The military takes control of Brazil, sets up dictatorship.

1975   Lula is elected president of Metalworkers' Union.

1979   The Workers' Party is formed.

1980   Lula is arrested for union activity.

1982   Lula is defeated in run for the governorship of São Paulo.

1985   Brazil's government returns to civilian rule.

1986   Lula is elected to the national Congress.

1989   Lula loses presidential election to Fernando Collor de Mello.

1994   Lula loses presidential race to Fernando Henrique Cardoso.

1998   He loses second presidential election to Cardoso.

2002   Lula wins election as the first working-class president of Brazil.

Burns, E. Bradford. *A History of Brazil.* New York. Columbia University Press. 1993.

Gerson, Mary-Joan, and Golembe, Carla. *How Night Came From the Sea: A Story From Brazil.* New York. Little Brown & Co. 1994.

MacLachlan, Colin M. *A History of Modern Brazil.* Wilmington, Del. Scholarly Resources Inc. 2003.

Morrison, Marion. *Brazil.* Austin, Tex. Raintree Steck Vaughn. 1994.

Page, Joseph A. *The Brazilians.* New York. Da Capo Press. 1995.

Pinheiro, Leonardo. *Brazil.* Victoria, Australia. Lonely Planet Publications. 2002.

Richard, Christopher. *Brazil.* London. Addison-Wesley. 1995.

page:

11: 21st Century Publishing
13: AP Photo/Dado Galdiera
17: © AFP/Getty Images
22: © Reuters/CORBIS
25: © Bettmann/CORBIS
29: © Reuters/CORBIS
35: Associated Press, AP
39: Associated Press, AP
42: © Reuters/CORBIS
44: © Reuters/CORBIS
49: Library of Congress, Prints
and Photographs Division
[LC-USZ62-74644]
55: Library of Congress,
American Memories Division
G5401.P3 1902.B7

58: Library of Congress,
American Memory Division
[LC-USF344-091285-B DLC]
64: © Julia Waterlow; Eye Ubiquitous/
CORBIS
73: © Bettmann/CORBIS
75: © Stephanie Maze/CORBIS
81: © Stephanie Maze/CORBIS
86: Associated Press, AP
99: © Stephanie Maze/CORBIS
103: Associated Press, AP
105: Associated Press, AP
110: © Keren Su/CORBIS
114: © Reuters/CORBIS
119: © Reuters/CORBIS

Cover: © AFP/Getty Images
Frontis: © AFP/Getty Images

JOHN MORRISON is a Philadelphia newspaperman and freelance writer and editor. He is the author of *Syria*, *Frida Kahlo*, *Cornel West*, and *Mathilde Krim* for Chelsea House Publishers.

ARTHUR M. SCHLESINGER, JR. is the leading American historian of our time. He won the Pulitzer Prize for his book *The Age of Jackson* (1945) and again for a chronicle of the Kennedy administration, *A Thousand Days* (1965), which also won the National Book Award. Professor Schlesinger is the Albert Schweitzer Professor of the Humanities at the City University of New York and has been involved in several other Chelsea House projects, including the series REVOLUTIONARY WAR LEADERS, COLONIAL LEADERS, and YOUR GOVERNMENT.